To MICHA~~EL~~
WITH BEST WISHES,

Fred Behrend

To Michael,
   So glad to share this with
you!

Larry Hanover

Rebuilt from Broken Glass
A German Jewish Life Remade in America

Shofar Supplements in Jewish Studies

Zev Garber, Editor
Los Angeles Valley College

Rebuilt from Broken Glass
A German Jewish Life Remade in America

Fred Behrend

with Larry Hanover

Introduction by Hasia R. Diner

Foreword by Dr. Ruth K. Westheimer

Purdue University Press
West Lafayette, Indiana

Library of Congress Cataloging-in-Publication Data

Names: Behrend, Fred, 1926- author. | Hanover, Larry, 1967- author.
Title: Rebuilt from Broken Glass: A German Jewish Life Remade in America /
    Fred Behrend and Larry Hanover; foreword by Dr. Ruth K. Westheimer.
Description: West Lafayette, Indiana: Purdue University Press, [2017] |
    Series: Shofar Supplements in Jewish Studies | Includes bibliographical
    references.
Identifiers: LCCN 2017012198
        ISBN 9781557537843 (hardback: alk. paper)
        ISBN 9781612495026 (epdf)
        ISBN 9781612495033 (epub)
Subjects: LCSH: Behrend, Fred, 1926- |
    Jews—Germany—Lüdenscheid—Biography. | Jewish refugees—New York
    (State)—New York—Biography. | Jews, German—New York (State)—New
    York—Biography. | New York (N.Y.)—Biography.
Classification: LCC DS134.42.B44 A3 2017 | DDC 940.53/18092 [B] —dc23 LC record
available at https://lccn.loc.gov/2017012198

Cover image credit: Seder plate used by the Behrend family since 1710. Photo by Tyler
Hanover. Stained Glass Background supplied by bee67 via iStock/Thinkstock. Broken Glass
Transparent Frame supplied by macrovector via iStock/Thinkstock.

To my daughter Evelyn and my son Andy, who are the reason I began writing down my stories and translating my family diaries. Also, to the memory of my parents, grandparents, aunts, uncles, and cousins, both those who perished in Europe and those who had the strength and courage to start new lives in a new country. With this book, we have accomplished the true spirit of the words b'chol dor vador (from generation to generation).

—Fred Behrend

To my wife Cheryl, son Tyler, and daughter Gabrielle for their encouragement and love, which has meant so much to me throughout the years, and for being there for me as I worked on this project. You are my world. Also to Mom and Dad for their never-ending support through the years.

—Larry Hanover

Contents

Image gallery follows page 70.

Foreword

When I like something, I literally end up sitting on the edge of my chair, and that was my position the whole time when reading Fred Behrend's book *Rebuilt from Broken Glass: A German Jewish Life Remade in America*. It's true that there have been many books about World War II, the Holocaust, and the murder of six million Jews, and it's also true that I lived through that era in Europe and so am far too familiar with what occurred. But this book has some unexpected twists and turns and is both moving and humorous, so that whether the reader is an expert or new to the subject, *Rebuilt from Broken Glass* will be a welcome addition to this particular bookshelf of stories.

Like others blessed with a little bit of luck, Fred and his family managed to flee Germany. But the path they took wasn't the usual one, as they ended up in Cuba, a place so much in the news today. After a time, they managed to make the next step and move to New York, but this circuitous route to join the large German Jewish community in upper Manhattan is what makes the story so worth reading—that and Fred's personal style and humor.

I have known Fred for 50 years. He was a close friend of my late husband. We have spent untold evenings together over dinner and coffee. But like so many survivors of the Nazis' plan to exterminate the Jews, Fred didn't talk that much about the details of his escape. We all had similar stories, and so when together, we preferred to talk about our life here in America or the future rather than dwell in the past. The memories always remain painful, no matter how many years have gone by, and to dwell on those memories means keeping Hitler and his awful atrocities that much more alive in our new lives. We who were there would like nothing better than to forget. And yet we can't, and I mean that in both senses of the word. Yes, it's impossible for us to forget what happened to us, but also we must not forget, because there are too many people who would like us to deny that these horrors ever took place. They say it's all propaganda, but we who were there know differently, and we owe it to those who perished to keep these memories alive.

Others talk about Holocaust fatigue—that there have been so many books written, so why read one more. Even I suffer from it from time to time, being asked to talk about my life when I'd prefer to talk about more pleasant things, like sex! I'm not going to say that Fred's book is as good as sex, but I will say that while there are tough parts to read, he's created a book that's readable, that is to say, that it teaches along the lines of the Torah, and does so with humor. We need to keep the story of the Holocaust alive in the hopes that it will never be repeated, and Fred Behrend proves to be a storyteller worthy of the task.

Dr. Ruth K. Westheimer, sex therapist, media personality
New York City
November 2015

Preface

בְּכָל דּוֹר וָדוֹר חַיָּב אָדָם לִרְאוֹת אֶת עַצְמוֹ כְּאִלּוּ הוּא יָצָא מִמִּצְרַיִם

(In every generation one must look upon himself as if he personally had gone out of Egypt.)

—Pesachim 116b

You shall therefore impress these words of mine on your heart and on your soul . . . You shall teach them to your children, talking about them when you sit at home and when you walk along the road, when you lie down and when you get up.

—Deuteronomy 11:19

Without memory, there is no culture. Without memory, there would be no civilization, no society, no future.

—Elie Wiesel

Passover is more than just a holiday for me. My mind hearkens back to the years spent in my grandparents' home, everyone dressed in formal attire—right down to the dark suits and top hats worn by my father and grandfather. My grandparents never had much money, but on Passover, we were all royalty. Though our immediate family was not large, we always had at least twenty people at our table as it was important that any travelers coming through our hometown of Lüdenscheid be able to celebrate.

Passover is inseparable from my own personal story. It sits deep in my soul and reaches back *b'chol dor vador*—from generation to generation. It is so vivid that it does more than remind me of long-ago ancestors. It creates images of them as real people with real stories with whom I share a heritage.

The flavors and smells of the ritual Passover Seder meal take me back in time, as we use the same recipes now as we did in Lüdenscheid and in the generations before. But nothing symbolizes that feeling of connectedness more than the pewter Seder plate that sits at the center of the table. The Behrends first used it in 1710, when my ancestor Jacob engraved it with the Hebrew words describing the parts of the ritual service. It has been used at the Behrend table for every one of the more than 300 years since, with only one period of interruption.

That came in 1939 when we were forced to flee for our lives. The Nazis threw my father into a concentration camp in November 1938, arresting him on Kristallnacht, the Night of Broken Glass. He was released on the sole condition that we leave Germany as quickly as possible. Our quota number to allow us into the United States would not come up for some time, so we fled to the only country that would take us—Cuba. The Germans confiscated any material objects of value. Our Seder plate was not taken, thankfully, and it would sit in storage with most of our other unseized possessions for a couple of years, even after we arrived in New York City upon being permitted entry, until we could afford to pay the fee to retrieve them.

That Seder in Cuba, when I was 12, was life changing. At our Seders in Lüdenscheid, only two parts of the service interested me. First was when we got to eat. Second was when we got to search for the *afikoman*, a piece of matzo (unleavened bread) hidden for the children to find, for which there was a chocolate bar as a reward. Now, however, like the Hebrews leaving Egypt, we had lived our very own Exodus. Sadness pervaded the room. But after reading the words b'chol dor vador in the haggadah (the book telling the story of Passover), my father, ever the optimist, lifted our spirits with a short speech. He reminded everyone that we had left with our most prized possessions—the children.

Ever since Cuba, it has been a tradition to stop for a speech at that same point in the service, which comes after making a sandwich out of matzo and bitter herbs to remind us of the difficult times that we left behind. I remember asking my father at that Seder in Havana who would lead it when he wasn't around anymore.

"Just as I was taught by my father, and you learned from me, you will teach it to your children one day," he said.

And he was right. When the mantle of the head of the Behrend family fell on my shoulders after his death in 1958, I took over leading the Seder. My children Andrew and Evelyn love Passover and Judaism as I do—I largely credit my late wife Lisa for instilling that—and now they handle much of the responsibility, although the speech remains for me.

Just as in Germany, close friends and relatives join through the years at our Seder to keep the meaning of Passover alive as well. But each year, I have come to recognize how much smaller we number around the table and how much of the rich history of my family is already gone. I developed a gnawing feeling that celebrating Passover and giving that speech was not enough. Each year I have vowed to do more to see that the generations that follow remain steeped in the traditions that were so important to my family, and sustained us through some of the worst moments in history. B'chol dor vador . . . how do I do more to make sure that the generations to come never forget from where they came?

Ten years ago, I moved from the home in which I raised my children to a new one in New Jersey to be closer to them and their families. With nothing but time on my hands, I embarked on a project: to translate the diaries into English of their grandfather, great-grandfather, and those of other Behrends dating back to the end of the fifteenth century. Because my descendants wouldn't be speaking German, it became critical for me to have an English version of this family chronicle. Translating the chronicle has not been an easy task, as I sat at my desk often for four or five hours at a time trying to interpret the difficult, old world German. Words that flowed so eloquently, particularly from my father's pen, sounded so much less so when translated.

As I embarked on this journey, I began giving lectures. Schools, men's clubs, sisterhood events, temple groups . . . anywhere where people were willing to listen to my stories, I was willing to tell them. Wherever I went, people told me, "You should write a book." I'd never been much interested in doing that, but suddenly, the words from the haggadah and Deuteronomy came together. I need to write these stories down. I need to make sure that all of the generations to come can hear about my life—our life. They need to hear about the Holocaust and to hear about our exodus. But, perhaps most importantly, they need to hear about how we thrived, not just survived. They need to learn and understand that in the face of adversity, their ancestors persevered.

Recently, I had the opportunity to speak at my granddaughter's school at the request of her world civilization teacher. One hundred and fifty teenagers sat in the auditorium as I recounted the story of my life in Germany and the fortunate escape of my family from the homeland that wanted us no more. I saw pride in the eyes of my granddaughter as I told her classmates about *her* legacy. I watched the faces of those classmates as they realized that history is never more than one generation away.

This book, in a way, is not only an extension of the chronicle but is also my haggadah. It is my Passover tale to be retold and remembered. By writing this book, I have now accomplished what I set out to do. As with my father and grandfather before me, and their ancestors as well, my stories are now safe, secure, and more importantly, preserved for the generations to come. I can hear my father's voice as he says, "Just as I would expect from you."

Acknowledgments

There are many people I would like to thank for their help in putting together this memoir. My children Evelyn and Andrew not only provided me with love and support, but also helped in many other ways. Evelyn, in particular, spent many hours reading this manuscript, remembering many stories that I had forgotten, and proofreading chapters. Andrew helped with the recollection of stories as well.

My dear friend Nikki Rosen has supported me in this long undertaking and had to put up with the countless hours I spent at my desk writing or editing stories. I'm very fortunate to have found such wonderful companionship at this stage of my life.

I have made many terrific friends in my lifetime, all of whose stories helped make this book what it is. What began as the "Boots and Poles" hiking and skiing club became the "Lake Oscawana Crowd" and has lived on with the next two generations as our children continue the friendships we began more than 60 years ago. Each of you have played an important role in my life, and therefore in the making of this book.

I want to thank my dear friend Ruth Westheimer, my friend of more than 50 years, for contributing the foreword to this book and allowing me to tell her tale of fleeing Germany. Chapter 8, "Tales of Other Escapes," contains stories told to me throughout the years from family members and friends and depended largely on letters, personal written recollections, and assorted clippings that they provided me so their stories could live on. I am grateful that cousin Hanna Jellin and friend Frank Lewin (both now deceased) as well as another friend, John Mann, provided such documents to me later in their lives.

I would like to thank Peter Froehlich and his excellent team at Purdue University Press for guiding us through the publication process and improving the book along the way. Also, I want to express my gratitude to Hasia R. Diner, the esteemed New York University scholar, for contributing the introduction to this book and placing my recollections into a historical perspective.

I would be remiss if I did not give special thanks to coauthor Larry Hanover, without whom this book would never have come to life. Larry, I thank you for encouraging me to tell my stories in a more public way, and for giving me a voice with which to allow my tales to live on. You have helped me to fulfill a lifelong dream—to ensure that my story and that of my family survives me.

The book *Lüdenscheider Jüdinnen und Juden 1690–1945*, written by Erich Kann und Matthias Wagner, was an excellent resource that filled me in on what Lüdenscheid and its Jewish community was like in my early years. I thank Matthias for providing the material and communicating about his research. I also am grateful to Congregation Ramath Orah for allowing me to use information from its website to tell the tale of how Rabbi Robert Serebrenik saved his congregants from the clutches of Adolf Eichmann and brought them from Luxembourg to New York City. My family gravitated to this warm congregation and its remarkable rabbi and joined soon after arriving from Cuba. For this book, Larry and I have verified historical information wherever possible through various resources, particularly the website of the US Holocaust Memorial Museum, as well as the archives of newspapers, particularly the *New York Times*. Attribution to such sources is provided throughout the book as appropriate. Last, I would like to thank Anita Shaffer, Larry's former editor at the *Trenton Times*, for her thoughtful edits and advice in the book's formative stages.

A Scholarly Introduction and a Call for Scholarship

Fred Behrend's memoir, *Rebuilt from Broken Glass: A German Jewish Life Remade in America*, will take a place on a small but impressive shelf of published memoirs written by Jews who, whether as adults or children, fled the Nazi onslaught and settled in the United States. Behrend, with his parents, underwent the trauma of, in the words of historian Marion Kaplan, descending steadily from "dignity to despair" in their beloved homeland, then desperately searching for a place of refuge, and ending up in America, in New York. They, like about 150,000 of their peers, German-speaking Jews whom the Hitler regime had stripped of their citizenship, managed to navigate restrictions, both German and American, manipulate bureaucracies, and cope with uncertainties, until they set themselves up in the United States. Behrend not only takes his readers through the family's sojourn in Cuba—a way station to America, their initial experiences of finding their first American apartment, locating their first American jobs, and learning to function in America, but he also goes beyond, describing his young adulthood and his experiences in the American military during World War II and into the postwar period, when he built a business, got married, raised a family, and the like.

Behrend will join his peers who have managed to write memoirs and get them published, all sharing in print their experiences, often harrowing, of living and leaving Germany in the years from Hitler's accession to power in 1933 until the early 1940s, when war blocked flight, and then settling in the United States. These books, as well as those which told similar stories but focused on immigration to Palestine, England, and other, smaller places of refuge, whether in the Americas, Asia, or Africa, allow contemporary readers to learn about Germany's Jews, those who decided that they had to leave their homes, fearing for their lives and futures, and managed to do so. We might consider these individuals to be multiple-times lucky.

They had the means, both financial and bureaucratic, to move to safety. They managed to rebuild their lives in new places, and then they got to tell their stories to a wide audience, reaching people who read the books they wrote. Fred Behrend, thanks to Purdue University Press, becomes part of this exclusive group.

The lovely foreword by his friend, sex-advisor Dr. Ruth Westheimer, also a Jewish refugee from Germany, will aid, no doubt, in garnering recognition for this book and that recognition will be well-deserved, even if someone not so famous is here offering some other prefatory words.

Rebuilt from Broken Glass does not need another foreword. I could hardly hope to compete with Dr. Ruth, who not only has known Fred Behrend for decades and ably writes about him here, but through her radio, television, and print presence, has for decades been reaching audiences that no mere academic historian like me could hope for. Rather, this memoir offers a moment in time for such an historian, a professor of American Jewish history, to make a pitch to scholars of the Jewish past to think about a new, barely explored, subject to write about.

Such histories, to be written, could draw upon the robust number of personal documents donated by the German Jews who settled in America, lived and worked there, raising children who, like Fred Behrend, became American—rather than German—Jews, yet retaining elements of their parents' heritage and who saw themselves as legatees of the German Jewish cultural fusion. Libraries, historical societies, and Holocaust resource centers around the country house many more memoirs, far exceeding the relatively small number which ended up in published form, accessible to the public between two covers of a book.

The published memoirs represent indeed a small fraction of the oral testimonies given by German Jewish refugees who came to the United States and then deposited in some research facility or another. Those oral histories and written personal documents owe their existence to the 1970s when, in response to a number of profound cultural shifts in American life, many of American Jews who endured Nazism came forward and brought their stories to the larger public. While some of this had begun much earlier, in the last third of the twentieth century a movement ensued which involved people, then entering their retirement years, beginning to share the details of what they had undergone. Jewish and general American institutions helped by sponsoring testimonies, collecting documents, and finding ways to disseminate them to the public.

Researchers, often under the auspices of Jewish communal groups, launched history projects which sought to identify and record the voices of the women and men who fled Germany as well as Austria and Czechoslovakia before the outbreak of the war but after the nightmare of the Nazis had been visited upon them. The oral histories and the texts provided in written form, whether housed in university libraries, in Jewish community buildings, or museums, contain rich and useful information about that tumultuous era. They provide poignant insights about the all too common need of human beings, including some like these women and men who had been well situated and comfortable in the homelands, to pick up and run, desperately seeking some new land which would take them in.

The passage of time has made the papers of so many organizations, clubs, and other institutions founded by America's Jewish immigrants from Hitler's Germany available to scholars. As these women and men faced old age and the inevitable attrition of sickness and death, and as their children and grandchildren, for the most part, English speaking, thoroughly integrated Americans, did not need, for example, the services of a German-speaking Jewish mutual aid society, the records of such communal bodies migrated to archives and libraries.

Just one such example might suffice. The archives at the University of Wisconsin-Milwaukee houses a substantial collection of the papers of the New Home Club, a local institution founded by those refugees who settled down in this very German city on the banks of Lake Michigan. Over the course of decades the New Home Club provided loans to members in need. It staged literary evenings and hosted lecturers. It organized picnics and other social gatherings, and yearly sponsored Passover Seders for its members and its children. It participated in larger Jewish community events in Milwaukee, interacting through these with the local Jewish population, nearly all of whom had come to America from eastern Europe decades before. When in the middle of the 1950s Milwaukee's Jews came together to build a new, modern Jewish Community Center, the New Home Club donated money to put up a plaque memorializing their families and friends who had been murdered by the Nazis.

Via the New Home Club the German Jewish refugees in Milwaukee connected to some of the national German Jewish organizations based in New York. It sent news of the club's doings to the *Aufbau*, the nationally circulating German language newspaper written by, for, and about the refugee community around the country. The leadership of the New Home Club reached out to Milwaukee political figures and through the club these new Americans engaged with some of the city's and the nation's most important events. A civil rights attorney, Tom Jacobson, whose parents belonged to the New Home Club, came to one of the meetings to inform his parents and their friends about the burgeoning struggle in Milwaukee for African American rights. Through the club these women and men who had so brutally lost their property at the hands of the Nazis learned how to negotiate the restitution procedures instituted by the government of the Federal Republic of Germany in the 1950s. It provided them with advice and legal services to try to recoup some of their losses. The club even served as something of a liaison with the German consulate stationed in Milwaukee and maintained occasional connections with some of the German non-Jewish institutions in the city.

All in all, the New Home Club papers offer snapshots of this one city, its Jewish population, and the life and concerns of the refugees from Nazi Germany. The records of the New Home Club, professionally stored in archival boxes in the University of Wisconsin-Milwaukee library, contain the names of members, their addresses, how much money they asked for when they needed help, the minutes of the board, summaries of the lectures, and press releases it sent to the local general and Jewish press, among so many other treasures for historians eager to study this time period, this place, and these people. Individual members shared details of their own harrowing experiences in Germany, their search for a place of refuge, and their early years in America.

The archival records, like the papers of the New Home Club and the many personal documents, varying in size from just a few pages to book-length, reside for the most part in archival boxes as well as in the file cabinets of research institutions. Strewn across the country, they are available for research, having for the most part been expertly preserved. Trained archivists have created indexes and finding aids to guide scholars or interested laypeople through the research process. Whoever has a chance to go to one of these archives, open one of the boxes, and scan the files will learn much about Jewish life in German-speaking lands before the war, the Jews' recognition of the Nazi threat, the frantic search for places of refuge, the multiple-stepped migrations, and then the laborious process endured by all of putting down roots in a new place. The transcriptions of the oral histories or the written memoirs which have been put away for safe-keeping in one scholarly repository or another nearly always chronicle the process of moving into a new dwelling place, learning a new language, figuring out how to make a living, making entreaties to Jewish aid organizations, forging new friendships, recreating community and culture, and the like.

Of the many research centers which have helped create this corpus of material, none looms larger or has played a more central role than the Leo Baeck Institute (LBI), founded in the mid-1950s as a living memorial to the Jews and Jewish culture of the German-speaking lands. Through its publications and annual meetings it has done an admirable job of making the refugees and their children aware of their own role as witnesses to a momentous historical event. LBI has helped make possible the recording and collection of such stories, and the hundreds of personal documents it collected. Evidence of German Jewry's flight from certain death to new homes in the United States have been available for decades for those researchers who could make the journey to its facility in New York, where, sitting in the reading room, they could peruse the details offered by the informants. Those informants commonly described their lives before the Nazis, their recognition, whether gradual or acquired all at once, that they and their families need to leave, the decision to flee, the often perilous and complicated steps in the journey, and finally settling down in one American city or another. Innumerable scholars have dipped into these materials. No doubt many nonscholars have done as well for their dramatic human interest value.

In the early twenty-first century the details of the lives of German Jewish immigrants who came to America in the 1930s exist broadly and widely and can be easily examined. The Leo Baeck Institute now, thanks to the bounty of digital technology, has rendered these very human stories, stories that we might think of as mostly quite triumphant, accessible to anyone, anyplace. "Digibaeck, German-

Jewish History Online" has taken these personal texts out of the archives and into the electronic devices of interested parties wherever they find themselves. So too the massive digitization of newspapers, particularly in this case of the American Jewish press, through such projects as J-Press, which makes it possible to read through local and national Jewish newspapers from the 1930s, 1940s, and beyond, which contain a trove of information about the German Jewish refugees, how they interacted with settled American Jews, most of them of east European parentage, and how they created clubs, centers, synagogues, and commercial establishments in one community after another. Additionally, the American Jewish Joint Distribution Committee, the body founded during World War I to aid Jews in distress and which played a crucial role in the settlement of the German Jewish refugees, has also put its massive records online. The stories of individuals and communities, of families and Jewish institutions can be unearthed, understood, and written about through these many sources.

Not only could a cadre of historians contemplating writing this history turn to Jewish research institutions or to archival collections of German Jewish organizations, but also the records of the many Jewish social service and help organizations, founded long before the 1930s, would yield much data to be mined. For example, many of the women among the refugee population received advice, guidance, and support from the National Council of Jewish Women. The organization was founded in the 1890s by women of the earlier German Jewish migration to America to provide family, household, and professional assistance. It created, for example, a special office to help refugee women who had been nurses in Germany and Austria as they negotiated the American licensing process. Those papers, with case records, statistics, and organizational information, exist, and an historian would find in them material for an almost self-obvious project on Jewish women, German Jewish newcomers, the American nursing profession, and the like.

Clearly I am making a case here that records exist in abundance, but despite the collection and publication of memoirs, we have not witnessed in any significant way the emergence of a serious and sustained scholarly enterprise to study these documents and to use them to ask some profound questions about Jewish life in central Europe before the war, the process of emigration, and most importantly here, the many issues involved in how these refugees adapted, adjusted—or did not—to their new lives in America. Not that no scholars have turned to these matters. Steven Lowenstein's *Frankfurt on the Hudson: The German-Jewish Community of Washington Heights, 1933-1938: Its Structure and Culture* (1989) stands as an exception. So, too, do scattered articles in the Leo Baeck Institute *Annual* that have over, the last few decades, treated some elements of this important historical phenomenon.

Before Lowenstein, Herbert A. Strauss, born in 1918 in Wurzberg, Germany, one of the refugees himself, published two volumes in 1978, *Jewish Immigrants of the Nazi Period in the USA*, which stand, along with Lowenstein's book,

as nearly the only published histories of the flight and settlement of the lucky
among Germany's Jews who made it to the United States. The volumes offer a
rich compendium of essentially unanalyzed data, a perfect starting-off point for
any scholar who realizes the richness of the subject.

This is not the place to analyze these works critically or to find fault with
them. They stand as important studies, although both could have extended their
chronological scopes. After all, the German Jews Lowenstein wrote about, who
settled in Washington Heights, continued to go through the process of identity
and institution building after 1938, when he brought his study to a close. They and
their American-raised and -born children engaged with multiple worlds, American, American Jewish, and that of the German immigrant enclave. How did they
balance these three? What kinds of career, political, and religious forces shaped
their lives into the war and postwar eras? How did they engage with New York City
and how did that change over time? How long did they, or their children, remain
in "Frankfurt on the Hudson"? Did they participate in the suburban migration of
so many other New York Jews? These and so many other questions suggest themselves from Lowenstein's book. And importantly, Lowenstein chose to not to look
beyond New York, or indeed beyond a single, albeit important neighborhood.

It had not been, at all, his obligation to answer these and other possible
questions which I am going to sketch out below. After all, like any scholar, Lowenstein defined a particular problem, an important one at that, and did a fine job
of answering it. He had no reason to ask a different question. But by thinking a
bit about what he did not do, it should become clear as to what subsequent scholars might have done, but heretofore have not.

Lowenstein did not extend his study beyond 1938, a crucial year for sure, but
still he offered a very limited time scope. Other scholars could have extended his
analysis into the years after Kristallnacht, when the Behrend family arrived in New
York's nearby Morningside Heights neighborhood, through the war and postwar
eras. How, they might have asked, did the immigrants or refugees, whatever we
may call them or whatever they called themselves, participate in Jewish communal
institutions and gatherings beyond Washington Heights? How did they engage
with German Jews in New York who came in the years before the scourge of Nazism? Did the children of the immigrants participate in youth activities outside of
the refugee enclave or did they serve as the ones to venture into the larger world
of New York Jewry? Where did they go to school and how did their educational
experiences bring them into contact with other Jews or non-Jews for that matter?
How many of the children, like Fred Behrend, entered the United States military
during World War II and how did that experience shape them? What happened
to the German Jewish families, shops, and other gathering places as the neighborhood, after the 1950s, attracted large numbers of immigrants from the Dominican
Republic? Did the children of the Washington Heights community marry from
within their tight-knit community or did they cross over and wed Jews of eastern
European background? Did the refugees rush to acquire citizenship, and if yes,

how did they behave politically in the rough-and-tumble of New York politics? These and so many other questions just about Lowenstein's subjects suggest themselves, or better, should have suggested themselves to historians who read his book.

Lowenstein's book and the two Strauss volumes, as well as the memoirs and the handful of scholarly articles which have appeared, here and there, over the course of the last few decades, we might think of as intellectual teasers, as lures which should have called upon others to pick up the torch and go further. What has been published so far, small as it is, should have enticed other historians, showing them how much material they could get their hands on, how rich the potential questions they could ask, and how important the topic could be to historians of America, American Jewry, and German history. These works contributed much, but should have blossomed into a full-fledged scholarly enterprise. They ought to have opened the door to a flood of other studies. It should have been obvious to any American or American Jewish historian, or even historians of the German Jewish experience interested in the era spanning the mid-1930s through the end of the twentieth century, that these immigrants' stories deserve to be studied. Indeed we might want to ask why no scholars, whether doctoral students looking for dissertation topics or established historians already ensconced in academic positions, extended and deepened this work. Why have so few historians trained their eyes on the many analytic problems that grow out of these early books and which suggest themselves when contemplating the experiences of the approximately 150,000 central European Jews who managed to escape to safety as Fred Behrend and his family did.

That question of why the topic has not taken root in the scholarly world lies beyond the scope of this short piece here. Rather, I would like to merely take note of the scholarly silence and use this, as my title indicates, as a "call" to historians to realize the width and depth of the source materials and how many fascinating and analytically rich questions arise. Historians in so many specialties have in recent decades articulated an interest in such overarching analytic themes as everyday life, gender, transnationalism, race, Diaspora, the history of emotions, the impact of trauma, the role of the state, and identity formation. Looking at the experiences of German-speaking Jews who fled their homelands after 1933 and came to America can provide a meaningful way to explore such issues.

My call here for a massive scholarly project on the German Jewish refugees in America, both in their own time and the trajectory of their children should not imply that no one has studied these immigrants—Lowenstein and Strauss aside—but even a brief perusal of the scholarship shows that what has been done merely skims the surface of the rich trove of material and seemingly endless questions that a scholar could ask. As such, I want to make note of a few specialized books and articles already published which have tackled some aspects of this large subject. The existence of these works confirm how much we still can learn from studying the German Jewish immigration to America and the role of these immigrants in America.

Gabriella Edgecomb, herself actually not an historian, in 1993 wrote a fascinating book, *From Swastika to Jim Crow*, which subsequently became a documentary film that explored the experiences of a small handful of German Jewish academicians, sociologists, psychologists, and anthropologists who managed to flee to safety by taking teaching positions at southern African American colleges. How they engaged with the American issue of race in the segregated South suggests multiple studies that could be done on other German Jewish refugees, not necessarily academics, who found homes in places like New Orleans, Charleston, Atlanta, and elsewhere in the world of Jim Crow. How, someone could study, did German Jews in northern cities come to terms with the color divide and what about the many other manifestations of American racial politics. How, for example, did German Jewish refugees on the West Coast respond to the internment of Japanese Americans into their concentration camps during World War II at the hands of the United States government? One could imagine that some may have been so bent on the defeat of the Axis power that they could justify such a racially based violation of constitutional rights, while on the other hand, others might have found the idea of relocations camps and internment centers as eerily familiar. We should remember that some of the refugees, like Fred Behrend's father, actually spent time in a camp. How might he or others like him have reacted to learning that the American government decided to perpetrate such acts on American soil?

Cornelia Wilhelm has recently embarked on a study of German Jewish refugee rabbis in the United States. She will document how they functioned within the context of the American rabbinate and the particular structure of American Judaism, so different from what they had known in Germany. Her work, in a relatively early stage, points out how much the realm of religion offers a rich way to think about the experiences of the German Jews in America in the period after their arrival in the 1930s. We do already have biographies of some of these men already, like Joachim Prinz, who escaped from Berlin, served as a rabbi in Newark, New Jersey, and came to national, indeed international attention, in August 1963 as he addressed the great March on Washington at which Martin Luther King Jr. gave his iconic "I Have a Dream" speech. We surely need more and need to know to what degree German-born, German-educated rabbis became part of local Jewish communal bodies. How did they participate in interfaith activities? How much did they share with their American congregants about their ordeals under Nazism?

The realm of religion should also provide fertile ground for scholars of American Jewish history to think about. Did the refugees or those among them who sought out organized religious life create their own congregations or did they join preexisting ones? If the latter, they by definition had to interact with American Jews, most of whom had come to the United States no more recently than the mid-1920s. How did the newcomers, the victims of Hitler's terror, engage with American Jewish congregational life? Did language prove to be a barrier?

While we have numerous biographies of a few very important German Jewish intellectuals who came to America and impacted the American world of ideas, inside and outside of academia, individuals like Hannah Arendt, Bruno Bettelheim, Leo Strauss, Hans Morgenthau, and others, we know relatively little about the less famous German Jewish men, and some women, who took up teaching posts at American colleges and universities teaching German language and literature. How did it feel to these once loyal Germans, lovers of German culture, but now victims, to teach this subject to American students? So too the life histories of individual German Jewish musicians, writers, and movie makers, many of whom ended up in Los Angeles have appeared, and entered into the scholarly and popular literature. However interesting and important these books, however recognizable these names, they do not go much further than the study of some famous person, doing famous work.

Those biographies however should point us to the reality that few of even those German Jewish refugees who went to California took up their careers in Hollywood or made their marks in literary circles. Rather most, more prosaically, although I would argue more interestingly, took up their American lives in shops and offices, opening small businesses, whether new or continuous, of the kinds of work that they had known back home. How did they do that? What steps did they take to open up grocery shops, electronics stores, cafés, bakeries, dress-making enterprises, and more? Who helped them out? Did the established Jewish charitable societies jump in to assist them? How did the arrival of the refugees in Los Angeles or Washington, D.C., in San Francisco or Baltimore, energize local Jewish communal bodies? Did those bodies have to reorganize in order to address the need? How did they balance the demands of the refugees with those Jews living there, still struggling with the economic straits of the (Great) Depression?

Making a living offers historians a rich subject for thinking about any group of people, including immigrants, particularly those who migrated under duress, and offers a particularly vivid way to understand their experiences. The historians willing to tackle German Jews who came to America as they escaped Germany would be able to find out how many went into self-employment and how many worked for others. Did they find employment with Jewish employers or did they work for non-Jews? How did language facilitate one kind of livelihood versus another, and importantly, what about their children and their career trajectories? Fred Behrend has much to say about this for himself, but what about the many others?

The analytic category of geography and place in America offers yet another unexplored way of thinking about this immigration, its structure, and its experiences. While so much of the literature, like Lowenstein's book and Fred Behrend's *Rebuilt from Broken Glass*, take place in New York, the Jews who escaped from Germany did not settle there, exclusively. Many of them found places to live and work through the aegis of Jewish relief agencies like the Hebrew Immigrant

Aid Society (HIAS). HIAS combed the country looking for communities where these newcomers could make a living, and as a result spots of German Jewish life planted themselves in all regions, in many states, settling in big cities and smaller towns. German Jewish life as such played itself out all over the United States and an historian, or several, would have much to work with in terms of charting those places, finding out what kinds of institutions they built and where, and how place size and proximity to New York—clearly the largest and most significant center—impacted German Jewish community life; integration, both into the Jewish and the American worlds; and generational change.

In terms of space as an analytic category, with the benefit of contemporary computer-generated research tools, it would be feasible for the historian to plot exactly where German Jewish refugees in say, Providence, Rhode Island or Allentown, Pennsylvania, lived. Did they find apartments or houses near one another? Did larger cities like Milwaukee or Cincinnati become home to actual neighborhood enclaves, and how long did they persist? Where they settled in mixed neighborhoods, among whom did they live, a readily answerable question which can be examined through US Census material? And in addition, in those places where German Jewish newcomers constituted a scant minority of the general or even the Jewish places, a set of questions suggest themselves that computer-generated data cannot answer. How did they interact with their neighbors and how did their neighbors engage with them? The historian could look at such formal and informal institutions as Parent-Teacher Associations, neighborhood and merchant associations, and see if the refugees joined and participated in these groups. How, again, did that change over time? Perhaps the entry of the United States into World War II and the widespread national effort to defeat Hitler made it increasingly comfortable for these immigrants to stake their place in their communities. All such questions, however, await the careful and creative efforts of historians willing to take them on.

Finally, a history of the German Jewish refugee world in America needs to think about the kinds of communal institutions the refugees built for themselves, independent of existing Jewish structures. I have already spent a bit of time here on the New Home Club in Milwaukee, a club whose papers I consulted for a book I wrote about post-World War II American Jews and the memorialization of the Holocaust. I know that similar clubs, as well as old age homes, mutual aid societies, and charitable societies, took shape as German Jewish refugees settled down in America. In their American world they also formed more informal groups, often although not exclusively for leisure. Again, Fred Behrend's description of the ski club he belonged to, made up of other young refugees, hints at a world worth studying.

They may have come fleeing violence and recognized that at home they faced certain doom. They made long journeys, like the Behrend family, and endured multiple stops in places like Cuba, the Dominican Republic, Haiti, Costa Rica, and Mexico, until they made it to the United States, where so many no doubt faced disorientation, bewilderment, and alienation. They had to embark on the arduous process of finding jobs and feeding their families, often doing so in positions far beneath their educations and the status they had enjoyed before Hitler. Yet references to German Jews even in the 1930s and 1940s, spending some time away from work in the Catskill Mountains, for example, hint at a strain of resilience and an ability to enjoy life again. Descriptions in Lowenstein and other works about cafés, where German Jewish women and men sat, drank coffee, ate cake, and socialized has great historic significance, and we need to know about that both as we seek to understand this migration in particular and also as we think about the millions of refugees on the move right now. How does this historical episode of refugee life provide a context for thinking of others?

What about their psychological adjustment to American life? What we know about their leisure activities suggest that these refugees figured out, no doubt imperfectly, how to pick up and start over in a new place, not dragged down by the traumas they had experienced. That, however, I offer purely as a supposition because we have nothing but anecdotes given here and there about mental breakdowns, unending unhappiness, even suicides. But which prevailed? How commonly did distress overpower the process of rebuilding? Records of Jewish social service agencies, staffed by social workers, could certainly provide some leads, as might hospitals in cities and neighborhoods where large numbers of the refugees clustered. The story cannot be only an upbeat one of adjustment but without close, deep, and careful empirical data, we frankly just do not know.

Finally, a call for a full-blown scholarly project on the history of the German Jewish refugee experience in America directs us to thinking about how these women and men expressed themselves at the time, how they described their lives, what they worried about and what they valued. Unlike the oral histories and memoirs like *Rebuilt from Broken Glass*, all written with the hindsight of the past as the authors look back and try to makes sense of their former selves, reading closely what people wrote at the time offers a very different perspective. All kinds of writing would be worth analyzing, whether documents intended only for family members or letters of request to charitable societies or government officials, all would offer a window into their concerns at the time. Did the clubs sponsor literary events where women and men wrote short stories or poetry? Did the synagogues they built have weekly or monthly newsletters to which the members contributed? All of these and many more would help in constructing a large picture of this particular American immigrant population and also would provide an intimate look into their lives.

In the context of this point I want to highlight one article on one written source, which in and of itself offers a universe of material, worth scholarly exploration. In 2013, Benjamin Lapp published an article in the *Leo Baeck Institute Yearbook*, "The Newspaper *Aufbau*, Its Evolving Politics and the Problem of German-Jewish Identity, 1939-1955." Lapp correctly identified this newspaper, written in German and launched in 1934, as a project of New York's New World

Club, the same name taken by the Milwaukee group. What began as a bulletin transformed into a newspaper which circulated around the United States. Fred Behrend served on the *Aufbau*'s board for 20 years and commented upon the publication in his memoir.

The *Aufbau*, as described by Lapp and referred to by Behrend, played a crucial role in the building of German Jewish community life and identity in America. It reported the news. It told German Jewish refugees living in Los Angeles, Cincinnati, St. Louis, Milwaukee, and New York, and so many other places too numerous to list here, about their peers around the country. It let them know who had arrived in America and where they now resided. The paper carried news about what kinds of synagogues, clubs, and mutual aid societies they had found and what activities they offered. It reported on births and deaths, on tragedies abroad, and successes in America. From the pages of the *Aufbau*, a newspaper truly transnational in scope connected the German Jewish refugee Diaspora across space, linking North America, Europe, Latin America, the Caribbean, Palestine/Israel, southern Africa, and the Antipodes. In all these places, those whom Hitler and the Nazis demonized and sought to destroy found new lives. The *Aufbau*, whether in its reportage of the news, its editorials and features, its personal announcements, letters to the editor, classifieds, or advertisements, encapsulated the many activities and concerns of the world of the Jewish refugees from Germany, in particular those who managed to reach American shores.

This call for scholarship might interest the general reader who picks up Fred Behrend's memoir. I hope it does. I hope that this brief piece of writing here has provided some of the larger context for his personal story and allows the reader to both relish what he has said and yet see that the issue far transcends this one individual. Clearly his experiences, however they are his alone, conformed to the outlines of a larger history which for the most part has been barely started, let alone exhausted. With the encouragement of Purdue University Press, I, however, wanted primarily to use this opportunity provided to me as a result of the publication of *Rebuilt from Broken Glass* to prod doctoral students and historians in the fields of German, Jewish, and American history to recognize that this subject represents a wide open, barely explored topic, which would tell us much about people under duress experiencing a nearly miraculous rescue and how they, by themselves and with the assistance of others who stepped forward to help, rebuilt their lives in new places. The topic would, I think I can promise, be rewarding because the plentiful sources dovetail so perfectly with the many questions that no one has yet posed. The story of these refugees as they became American and American Jews awaits the attention of some group of future historians ready to tackle the narrative of this endlessly fascinating cohort and their moments in Jewish and American time.

Hasia R. Diner
New York University

CHAPTER 1

Growing Up in Germany

Most children love a parade. I certainly did growing up in Lüdenscheid, a city tucked in the mountainous regions of western Germany, in the early to mid-1930s. I vividly remember the parades that accompanied the *Schützenfest*, or sharpshooting contest. They marked the start of this grand festival held every May, where cities and states would compete with one another at the local range, then celebrate in the park with prodigious amounts of beer, sausages, and music.

My parents never took me to see the competition, but I was thrilled just to watch the Nazi stormtroopers march past my parents' store on the way up to the top of the hill where the tree-lined park and shooting range were located. The men were so impressive in their brown shirts and trousers and Nazi armbands, marching in perfect formation to musical accompaniment by drums and trumpets. As they goose-stepped along, legs raised high with each step, the rhythmic stomp of their black combat boots echoed through the streets. Bright red banners, with black swastikas emblazoned in the center, were held high and snapped in the breeze. The men gave the *heil Hitler* salute to residents lined along the parade route, and we returned the salute in kind.

I remember what I would say to my father, Herman Behrend, and my mother, Else, as we went outside for this spectacle.

"Aren't they great?" I asked. "When I grow up, maybe I can march with them."

They just let my comments go without a word. After all, they couldn't say anything without endangering us. Anybody within earshot could be an informer, someone who would run to the *Gauleiter* (local Nazi Party chief) to say that an individual refused to give the Nazi salute or criticized the regime. Being Jewish, of course, meant we were all the more vulnerable to reprisal.

It was only as an adult that I realized how sheltered I was. I only knew what my parents told me of the outside world. I was so protected from the terror of the Nazis' increasing persecution of Jews that I didn't realize I should dread, not admire, their parades until after my father was arrested in 1938 and thrown into a concentration camp. It was a lost childhood.

But if you're going to have a lost childhood, you might as well enjoy it. It's much easier to lead a sheltered existence with a family that has money than one that doesn't. We might have been poor by the time the Nazis were done plundering our possessions, but my family worked hard, and, as a result, we were well off when I was a kid.

In my family's eyes, there was clearly nothing unusual about Jews attaining wealth and respect in our beloved Lüdenscheid. We were Germans first, Jews second.

Germany was an enlightened society where a man was judged by his character and how charitably he performed in his community—or in my father's case, even singing in the traveling Lüdenscheid choir in a group that was otherwise all non-Jews. I wasn't completely blind at my age to the antisemitism going on around us. I saw the occasional signs ridiculing "filthy Jews" at the storm trooper parades, telling people not to buy from Jewish-owned stores. But there were always people who scorned Jews throughout history. It was nothing to worry about. My parents certainly didn't seem worried and never intimated that Jews were singled out more than anyone else was. Like any child, I took my cues from them. Even if I couldn't attend public school anymore, as the Nazis passed more anti-Jewish laws by the week, this, too, was just a temporary circumstance. The storm would pass, the Nazis would settle down, and things would eventually return to normal.

For me, normal meant being spoiled rotten. I'm sure you've heard of the word "zeppelin." That's what they called airships long before the Goodyear blimp took over and started circling above Super Bowls. Zeppelins were a popular, luxurious form of travel back in those days, up until the Hindenburg disaster in 1937. Well, they got their name from the inventor and manufacturer of the original airships, a man named Count Ferdinand Graf von Zeppelin.

My parents were not as successful financially as Graf von Zeppelin, who had maintained a residence in Lüdenscheid until his death in 1917. But their store was successful enough in selling silk for ladies' clothing and linens that they were able to rent Zeppelin's compound. The best way I can describe the size of the grounds and how self-contained it was is to compare it to the Kennedy compound in Hyannisport, Massachusetts. It didn't have an oceanfront, of course, but beyond that, the comparison isn't far off. We not only had an enormous house and other buildings for servants, but also a pond with ducks and swans, as well as two fountains full of little fish. We also had a greenhouse, where the gardener grew beautiful flowers during the long winter months, and a bountiful vegetable garden. It was there, amid lush grounds full of apple and cherry trees, that I lived from the time I was six years old.

The gardener and his wife lived on the premises. There were other domestic employees as well, including a cook and a maid, and an employee who would come over from my parents' store to serve as chauffeur as needed.

The house had one other significant feature. The iron fences and brick walls were anywhere from six to twelve feet high. Even the double gates were nine feet high; it took two people to open them when we drove in to park the automobile. But even though this house was a Garden of Eden, it was a prison for a young boy. This house and those walls are the reason that, even today, my memories of childhood in Germany are so relatively few, containing so little in the way of meaningful interactions with other children. Sometimes I wonder if I was better off that way, given the frightening nature of what was going on around us. Looking back, I suspect if I were in my father's and mother's shoes, I would have handled the situation the same way. Childhood is a time for play, not for being exposed to the real world.

Some parts of life in the Zeppelin house I could have done without. One of the girls who worked in our store was a champion cross-country skier from our province of Westphalia. My father insisted that she take me out twice a week to show me how to cross-country ski, especially because admission to public school was contingent on being proficient enough at skiing to get there. I hated every minute of my lessons, although the gardens were so large that there was plenty of room for practice. Fortunately, there was downhill skiing in Lüdenscheid, which was much more fun. I loved to go with my father down its slopes, which were a popular destination for skiing enthusiasts. Lüdenscheid was even one of the few cities to boast a ski jump, which people used to practice for competitive events. When my father asked if I would like to go jumping with him, I said, "Oh, you first." There was no way I was going airborne.

As for me as a young boy, if I asked for something, I usually got it (I suppose that's the definition of "spoiled brat"). I used to have a train set that far exceeded what you would consider a toy. The railroad ran through the second floor of the house with the engines steaming around and around. One day, my father brought home a giant chest of miniature bricks used by architects to build models of buildings and homes. We worked them into the railroad system, constructing various bridges, cathedrals, temples, and towers.

As you can imagine, any young boy left to his devices in such a house might be prone to mischief. I remember borrowing the gardener's bicycle and trying to navigate three flights of steep stairs from the upper level of the garden to the street below. I was found unconscious at the bottom, bruised and bleeding, with his bicycle totaled. It was only the sight of my pitiful state that saved me from a good spanking. The property provided other challenges as well. My parents never understood why they would encounter so many broken glass ceiling tiles at the greenhouse, although I suspect it might have had something to do with my efforts to determine how many I could walk across before they cracked or shattered. They also could not figure out why the fountain was always short of goldfish. I'll never tell, although I must say that I still enjoy deep-sea fishing to this day.

Some of my favorite memories are of our vacations to Bückeburg, where my father grew up and his parents still had their home until they died in the early 1930s. Bückeburg was the capital of a small German state called Schaumburg-Lippe. It has a castle that you could describe as a feudal manor dating to the 1300s, with outer buildings, lush gardens, a pond in the courtyard, and a majestic inner structure. I felt like I practically grew up in those castle gardens, playing in the flowers and finely manicured shrubbery and lawns. It felt perfectly natural to wander in such beautiful, luxuriant grounds and play in what other children could only dream of.

Rhaden, where my mother's parents grew up, was a fun vacation destination, too. My memories of Rhaden are less vivid, but there are always certain memories that stick in your mind from childhood no matter how much time passes. They had no indoor plumbing. Instead, there was an outhouse where you would freeze your rear end off during the winter. They also had no running water and had to get water each day from a pump inside the house. The maid filled buckets and heated the water on a coal-heated stove before placing it in the tub for hot baths. It would be many years before twentieth-century conveniences made their way to rural towns like Rhaden, even for the well-to-do.

But at the Zeppelin compound back home in Lüdenscheid, for me, outside contact was minimal. I worked hard to burrow my way out here and there to see what it was like outside my gilded prison. When my mischief left me grounded in my second-floor bedroom, I would climb out the window, grab on to the solid branch of the oak tree sitting just outside, and make my escape over the fence. Those escapes, however, never translated into meaningful friendships beyond the walls. In fact, in one instance, it was quite the opposite. I did have one occasional playmate who lived right outside the walls of our house, Wolfgang Brinker, but even our interaction ebbed as the Nazi influence grew stronger and his parents kept him away from me. Another boy living right outside those walls, in fact, was quite the opposite of a friend.

His father, Walter Borlinghaus, was the Gauleiter, the head of the Nazi Party in the district. He and his wife actually behaved decently to us. But their son, Max, or "Mecki," must have been the pride of Adolf Hitler, serving as my introduction to antisemitism. I stayed away from his wall. He used to throw stones over it, and he would say, "I will kill you, you *Judenschwein* [Jewish pig]." The only good thing about him is that, from what I learned in later years, he did not survive the war. He gave his life to the Führer and the fatherland on the battlefields of Russia. A just reward. His father rose in the party ranks and in 1944 became a deputy in the Reichstag (the German parliament) before he shot himself in the final weeks of the war, according to various sources.

Mecki wasn't the only one to call me Judenschwein. As the 1930s progressed, German antisemitism grew more overt. When you met someone on the street, you were not greeted with a handshake or a *guten tag* (good day) but with a raised arm and a *heil Hitler*. But I could accept that there were some people who just didn't like Jews, because there were plenty of others who treated my father and mother with the utmost esteem and friendship. I didn't know to be frightened or intimidated by Nazis.

ॐ

To understand the shock that my family experienced as Germany turned against its Jews, you have to understand the history of my family. We can trace the roots of the family Behrend back to the 1490s, when Christopher Columbus sailed for America. Even into the early 1900s the family's ancestral home in the city of Rodenberg still stood as it had for three centuries. Jews had never been allowed to ascend in government or business as their gentile counterparts had and were not allowed citizenship. But I know many people who cannot trace their ancestry back even more than a century, let alone half a millennium. Why shouldn't we feel as German as anyone else after so many years in the land? I was taught to be proud of my heritage and I still am today.

As Germany advanced into the twentieth century and became more modern, a Jew like my father Herman could advance even more—and did. He was a patriot. He would give and do anything for the fatherland. To me, he could do virtually no wrong. He was the epitome of what a good German and a good man should be.

My father was born in 1883, and as a boy growing up in Bückeburg, he was a soldier at heart. For his birthday, my grandparents would give him soldier paraphernalia such as a wooden sword and a rifle. If I enjoyed watching the Nazi storm troopers parade by my house as a little boy, perhaps it was because of how he used to tell me about his biggest thrill as a child—marching along the parade route (on the side, of course) with Bückeburg's beloved Seventh Ranger Regiment, known as the Royal *Bückeburger Jaegers* (Hunters).

On the day that World War I began, on August 1, 1914, my father volunteered his services to his beloved elite *Jaegers*. He was heartbroken when they did not offer him a spot, and he had to settle for membership in the cavalry in the nearby city of Minden, on condition of providing his own horse. Because my grandparents were poor, the Jews of Bückeburg pooled their resources so he could have a horse and be able to accept the high honor of this commission. The next day, his thirty-first birthday, he found himself on a transport to the western front. Upon arrival, his regiment was greeted by a squadron of French bombers, suffering quite a heavy loss of men as well as horses—including his own brand new horse. I never found out how, but he managed to replace the horse without seeking more funds from the Jews of Bückeburg.

With his second horse beneath him, my father was able to keep campaigning. He was wounded twice but was able to return to action. Over the four years of the war, he fought on the front lines in France, Galicia (now part of modern-day Poland and Ukraine), Montenegro, and Turkey before being discharged after the armistice of 1918. For his service, he was awarded the Iron Cross first and second class and several other medals. Fighting in the army from the first day of the war to the last, my father proved beyond doubt his devotion to the fatherland.

This role played by so many Jews in World War I is critical to understanding why Jews felt they could be safe in Germany even as the Nazis rose to power. The war had forged a bond of brotherhood. It was real, not imagined. Betrayal of that bond could not happen all at once. And in my father's keepsakes is proof that the nation could not deny the achievement of its Jewish veterans, even as Hitler's antisemitism was weaving its way into its fabric.

In 1934, my father received the Cross of Honor medal that was awarded to all World War I front line veterans and accompanied by a certificate. In bold letters at the top, the certificate presented in the name of the mayor of Lüdenscheid ironically stated that he was giving it "in the name of the Führer and Chancellor of the Reich." A Jewish Telegraphic Agency article from July 1934 reveals that this was one of the rare instances where Paul von Hindenburg, the renowned but aging former field marshal who still served as president after appointing Hitler as chancellor in January 1933, prevailed over the Führer. It said Hitler insisted to Hindenburg that only Aryans receive the cross, but Hindenburg "sternly opposed Hitler's demand" and proclaimed all war participants were entitled. That allowed 96,000 Jewish veterans as well as parents and widows of 12,000 Jewish soldiers who died in battle to receive the award.

The story of my mother, born Else Oppenheim in 1885, also shows how even a young Jewish woman could build a life as a German citizen. She grew up in Rhaden, where her parents owned a store, selling clothing and linens to the local farming community. They lived on the top floor of the two-story store, which sat in a place of prominence, on the grounds of Rhaden's town plaza; the only other large building was a church, accompanied by a number of houses. My mother was sent off to a boarding school where, besides reading, writing, and math, she learned how to behave in society, being taught how to set a table, sit like a lady, and so on.

Like my father, her story is entwined in World War I. In March 1914, my mother married her first husband, a man named Robert Stern. Like my father, Stern, too, entered the service on August 1, 1914, the first day of the war. Just over a month later, Stern became the first Lüdenscheid resident to give his life for his country. After less than six months of marriage, my mother, at the age of 29, was a widow.

Before the war, Stern had operated a store in Lüdenscheid that bore his name and dealt in textiles. She was now the sole heir of the business and became its proprietor—something virtually unheard of for a woman in the early 1900s. Though new to the business, my mother applied herself to learning it. For the next several years, she not only operated the business alone, but also demonstrated that a woman could do so successfully.

As for my father, after the war he returned to a tiny village called Nieheim, where in 1912 he had begun managing a business catering to the daily needs of the farm community, delivering everything from clothing to tools via horse and buggy. Then, in 1922, my mother's parents began to send out inquiries to find their Else a second husband. In eastern Europe, as many know from *Fiddler on the Roof*, families used to engage the services of a matchmaker. But in Germany, things were done differently. Feelers were sent out through the region to locate someone who was Jewish and came from a good family. Money wasn't as significant a factor back then. It was your standing in the community—and your family's standing—that counted. My father was eventually requested to introduce himself to my mother. They were engaged in December 1922, and two months later, in a ceremony in my mother's parents' home in Rhaden, they were married.

Looking back, even their honeymoon foreshadowed what was to come in Germany. The Weimar Republic, as Germany was known after World War I, was paralyzed by a weak economy beset by massive inflation and unemployment, conditions that eventually would let the Nazis' tactics of scapegoating Jews take root. For their honeymoon, my parents went to Berlin on a buying trip for the Lüdenscheid store, which retained its original name of Robert Stern. They were forced to cut their trip short as the nation's runaway inflation reached its peak. Even with suitcases full of cash, they realized they were in danger of running out. They paid 15,000 marks for their hotel room on the first night. On the second night, it was 23,000 marks. It would have been 30,000 marks had they stayed for the third. There was only enough money for my mother to have a light snack on the trip home.

My parents' first child, a boy, was born on January 4, 1924. Sadly, he died shortly after birth. But on November 3, 1926, I was born and given the name Fritz Bernhard Behrend. I was a frail child, and the bris, or ritual circumcision, was held on the fourteenth day instead of the eighth day that is commanded in the Torah. At this point, my father was 43 and my mother was 41, so they delighted in this long-awaited event. My father held me for the ceremony, and my paternal grandfather, Gotthelf, was my godfather. Relatives and friends from across Germany came to join the festivities.

Shortly after I was born, a competitor to my parents' store bought out a nearby department store and opened in time for the Christmas season. The store was large and well-known in the industry and could have posed a threat to my parents' business. However, my father, who since their marriage ran the store with my mother, was a smart businessman. Rather than go head to head with the competitor, he went against the wishes of my mother and cleaned out all of their stock except for bedding, dress material, and silk fabric. They reopened the store as a specialty house for silk and ladies' fabrics, and then built an addition for the store where the bedding part of the business was housed.

I loved that store, particularly the bedding. Back then, feathers were big business. Duvets and pillows were all filled with feathers, and part of my parents' business involved cleaning these feathers. The local farmers would take the feathers out of the bedding and they would be placed inside a large machine, perhaps nine feet tall. I would gaze awestruck as the machine twirled the feathers around and around. Water or steam was added, and then the feathers were dried. Finally, they went through a large funnel-like machine that placed them into new duvets and pillows. Selling feathers was as big a business as cleaning them. There were many different grades. Goose down bedding was superior to chicken feathers, and feathers from the bottom of the goose were better than those from the top because they were warmer.

Soon enough, Robert Stern was the best-known store of its kind in Lüdenscheid and the surrounding area and it thrived. My parents built up to a staff of eight to ten employees, not to mention the household employees at the Zeppelin property.

℘

When I moved to America, I learned quickly that status was mostly about money. But for somebody who only knew patriotism and devotion to civic duty as the German path to esteem, this was a shock.

My father learned about serving the community from his father. Gotthelf Behrend's small manufacturing business, known as Bückeburg National Peasant Costumes, was liquidated when my father was 13. He then tried his hand at insurance, but for the rest of their lives, he and my grandmother barely scratched out a living.

Yet respect for my grandfather in Bückeburg was unbounded, largely because he cofounded the town's volunteer fire department, serving for 60 years and holding a title of honorary president. I had not yet turned six when my grandfather died in 1932 at the age of 81. But while other recollections of Germany have faded with the years, the funeral and ceremonies honoring my grandfather remain etched in my mind, supplemented by my own father's recollection, as detailed in his journal.

The fire brigade came and insisted that his coffin be placed in the pumper truck. It was drawn by six horses for a march through the city. Twelve comrades served as pallbearers, placing his remains in the truck. The department's band played Chopin's funeral march and his comrades marched in full firefighting uniform with torches. Finally, they arrived at the Bückeburg synagogue, where his body lay in state. The Nazis were gaining in power and the ascension of Hitler to chancellor was less than a year away. The Nazis' anti-Jewish rhetoric was on the rise. But Jews and non-Jews alike followed the procession through the whole city to the Harrl mountain ridge, where a small cemetery sits amid a grove of tall pine trees. Although I was too small to remember, another march through town, only festive, was held three years earlier, on October 22, 1929, to celebrate my grandparents' fiftieth wedding anniversary. It was said at the anniversary celebration that an honor of this kind was given to no one except the prince of Schaumburg-Lippe himself.

I am certain that such honors would have been bestowed upon my father as the years passed had Germany turned away from Nazi madness. Above the ancestral home of the Behrends were carved the words, "Let he who is in need, enter. He will find help and comfort here." My father honored those words. He and my mother accommodated both sets of parents for lengthy visits throughout the year. My father's parents survived financially largely because they stayed as guests in our house for several months at a time and received an annual stipend of 3,000 marks from my parents.

Like my grandfather, my father participated in all aspects of civic affairs, including a *Gesangverein*, or traveling chorus, that brings to mind the movie *The Sound of Music*. Once Christopher Plummer and Julie Andrews had fallen in love and she gave up the nun business, much of the film revolved around the von Trapp family's participation in a singing competition. It was considered crucial for the honor of Austria. Well, my father's participation in his Lüdenscheid singing group was along those lines. Mostly his group sang within the city limits, but from time to time, they would compete with others from various cities for the honor of their hometown in a songfest. He sang in the group of 20 or 30 men even though he was the only Jew.

Afterward, they would go to the local tavern, where some would drink themselves under the table. No wonder he was well liked, with more gentile friends than Jews. He could drink beer with the best of them.

My father even looked the part of a true German. He was six feet one, stood straight as a ramrod, and had blond hair and blue eyes—all features that made him appear the quintessential Aryan.

In fact, during parades throughout the year for war veterans, he would march right along with his comrades as head of the Lüdenscheid Jewish War Veterans. They had to walk behind the city's other veterans, but he marched proudly, wearing his old army uniform and saber. But he didn't just march. He stood at the front carrying the flag, at the request of his fellow comrades. He did this before and after Hitler came to power. At least once or twice, he carried a flag bearing the Nazi swastika. My mother admonished him, saying, "Herman, how can you carry that flag? No more, you don't do this anymore."

No one was particularly concerned that my father owned his saber and displayed it at the time. He had his large sword, the kind worn by an officer, and a smaller dagger as well. They were beautiful pieces with silver handles and worth considerable money. No one cared about his pistols, either. Even the police knew about his stash of swords and guns. They didn't care.

There is one more story that I would like to share to illustrate a mindset that he had—and he was not alone among German refugees, although frankly, I could never understand it. Let me fast-forward a moment to December 1944, after we had settled in New York. I was finishing high school and soon would be drafted into the US Army.

Against the advice of his generals, Hitler had ordered one last, desperate offensive against the Allies along the Western front, gouging their lines as they marched through the mountain forests of France and Belgium. It would be known as the Battle of the Bulge. The Allies eventually repulsed the surprise attack, but initially, the Germans made significant advances.

I remember my father reading the *New Yorker Staats-Zeitung*, a German-language newspaper that is still published today, and seeing the news that the Germans were surging into Belgium and France. Then he'd look me straight in the face and proudly say, nodding in approval, "Well, now, look at us Germans. Look what we are able to do!"

I was 18, hoping the war would still be on whenever I was drafted so I could avenge my father. Yet here he was, thinking like a German first, a Jew second. "Papa," I said, "how can you talk like that? They put you in a concentration camp. They ripped all the medals off your chest, asked you where did you steal them? And here you have the nerve to tell me, 'Look at us Germans'?"

But it was the same for him as with many others who escaped Germany. When they discussed Germany, somewhere in the conversation would leak a certain feeling of pride of what Germany used to be. You couldn't take that away from them.

Even though his German pride came first, he was a religious man committed to his faith. He was head of the Lüdenscheid congregation for many years, lodging, feeding, and entertaining all who came on congregational business. Our house and garden were frequently a center for happy social gatherings, accommodating friends as well as neighbors. Such was his stature in Lüdenscheid that my parents' store was able to survive for several years after the Nazis took power in 1933. The people of Lüdenscheid didn't buy the Nazi rhetoric about Jews being a cancer to German society. They ignored the Nazis for the most part and kept right on shopping, knowing my parents for the respectable business owners they were. What came out of Berlin or from the local Gauleiter, as opposed to what they saw before their eyes in Lüdenscheid, were two different things. But no Jewish business could survive for long under the propaganda onslaught.

☙

The Nazis first targeted the Jews on Saturday, April 1, 1933. It was named the official Day of Boycott against Jewish businesses and professionals. Stormtroopers from the SA and SS stood in front of Jewish-owned stores and banks, as well as the offices of professionals such as doctors and lawyers. Individual smaller towns and cities had to import Nazi Party members from other larger cities because unit members from the local towns were frequently too ashamed to participate. Violence occurred at some establishments throughout Germany, with police usually standing by without intervening.

The Robert Stern store was among those affected. My parents did not stand idly by. In one of our storefront windows, my parents displayed the picture of the founder of the store. Below it was a sign explaining that Robert Stern was the first soldier to die in the Great War from the city of Lüdenscheid and that the establishment's owner was his widow. Also placed in public view was a plaque honoring Stern, stating, "The gratitude of your fatherland is with you forever," along with a document, signed by the mayor, certifying the plaque's authenticity. So many members of the public assembled in front of the store that it became necessary to close the street to traffic. Representatives of the Nazi Party and the local police called my father and asked him to remove these articles from the window for the protection and safety of the public. My father took the hint and removed them.

It was a frightening day for the Behrends all the way around. My 80-year-old paternal grandmother, Mathilde Behrend, had just undergone a difficult operation and lay in the bed of a private clinic, near death. What's more, I was scheduled for my first day of public school. My mother sobbed uncontrollably. She never felt it was an option to keep me home or delay that first day of school, but she was fearful for my safety. The teachers, fortunately, were not members of the Nazi Party and assured her they would be honored to protect and take care of her little Fritzchen. My mother was grateful and was able to calmly leave her little six-year-old and head home.

Clearly, antisemitism did not represent the will of the people at this point. Not only did my teachers treat me well, but on the following Monday, my parents' business and other Jewish establishments experienced record sales volumes. Under these circumstances, it was reasonable for the 20 to 30 Jewish families in Lüdenscheid to hold out hope. In fact, Jews and non-Jews throughout Germany wondered whether Hitler, an upstart politician from Austria, could long stay in power. They assumed Hindenburg would return to the primary position of power. Instead, his health declined, he ceased to be a factor, and the president's post was eliminated upon Hindenburg's death in 1934. Hitler's power was complete.

As the months passed, the propaganda machine of Joseph Goebbels continued to cast blame on the Jews for everything that had ever gone wrong in Germany. The harangue of his speeches and of other officials continued at an increasing pace. After a while, when a people is exposed to lies long enough, the lies begin to seem like the truth. Citizens become brainwashed, and the poison spreads and begins to take root. It wasn't just the speeches. It became perfectly normal to see signs out on the streets with such slogans as "Destroy All Jews" (*Juda Verrecke*) or "The Jews are the Cause of our Misfortunes." These signs were hung on trees and telegraph poles and attached to advertising pillars, railroad cars, and even toilet facilities. The Nazis spread the vitriol through *Der Stürmer*, a must-read newspaper for party members edited by Julius Streicher, which, of course, all good Germans were encouraged to view.

Year after year, more antisemitic decrees came, eventually numbering in the hundreds. Aryan manufacturers were forbidden to continue to supply Jewish firms with merchandise or to purchase raw materials from Jewish factories. Civil employees and laborers were threatened not to make any purchases in Jewish establishments, and were told they would be fired without notice and lose their rights to a pension if they did. When these threats failed to have the desired effect, they were enshrined into law.

In September 1935, the Nazis enacted the Nuremberg Laws pertaining to the "reviled race." These laws meant that Jews, who for many years had grown comfortable in their role in German society, were no longer even citizens of the Reich. Suddenly, whether one was a practicing Jew or not made no difference. Anybody with three or four Jewish grandparents was officially branded as a Jew, even if they were practicing Christians. Those with one or two Jewish grandparents were considered *mischling*, or mixed blood. Jews could not marry Aryans, and physical or sexual contact with Aryans was strictly forbidden, punishable with time in jail. German maids under the age of 45 were no longer permitted to work in Jewish households, which affected my parents' ability to find help. Not a week went by without the jailing of numerous Jews.

These laws and decrees are only things that I know about in retrospect from history books and conversations over the years. If you asked me when I was a child to explain what the word antisemitism was, I wouldn't have had the slightest idea. Looking back, I suppose I considered Jews to be no more singled out in Germany than blacks, Hispanics, or any other racial or ethnic group in the United States are today. Even with Mecki, the Gauleiter's son who taunted me by calling me Judenschwein, I just couldn't understand that it was something that perhaps I should have taken to heart. The idea of being Jewish seeped through so rarely. I do remember overhearing my mother saying a woman had called them up, asking whether my parents could leave the back door of the store open. The woman wanted to make her purchases without anyone seeing her enter a Jewish store and possibly reporting her.

By 1936, amid the decrees and residents' fears of buying from Jews, the fortunes of my parents' business and those of other Jewish enterprises began to decline. By the time 1938 arrived, any thought of being able to remain in business had vanished. After a number of discussions, my parents reached the decision to hold a liquidation sale on June 15. They began to take inventory of the store's stock, and after eight days received permission to begin the sale. The sale required considerable preparations. First, my parents had to find enough salespeople to conduct it. With the help of a friend who loaned a few employees, my parents eventually had 20 on board for the big day.

When June 15 arrived, the mobs were frightening. I guess the word "sale" more than compensated for the word "Jew." The rush continued for four days. Only after a total of eight days was there a significant decline in the number of customers. The sale continued for the next two months, entering a renewed frenzy in its final days as my parents began offering leftovers and remnants. My parents were forced to end the sale on August 15 when the city administration denied a request for an extension. By that point, only 5,000 marks' worth of stock remained unsold. Even with the official sale over, however, the transactions continued to a lesser extent as my parents brought their leftover merchandise home and kept going in secret. They felt certain that our old and loyal customers would not give them away and were proven right.

My last year attending public school was 1937, as a Nazi decree forced Jewish children to be educated outside of what were now exclusively Aryan premises. The only Jewish school was in Cologne, some 65 miles away, but my parents had no other choice. They would have to find me a place to stay in Cologne so I could attend. After a prolonged search, my father arranged for me to live with the family of Max Baum at Jülicher Strasse No. 19. Baum was the cantor of the oldest and grandest synagogue in Cologne, an Orthodox temple called Glockengasse. Cantor Baum was a man of small stature but a deep, rich voice. I would often sit with his wife and two children around the piano to sing with him.

But parting from my parents filled me with anxiety. I had been sheltered for so long, but the neighborhood children at my public school had been urged by their parents not to be friendly with a Jewish boy, not to mention that my parents discouraged me from having neighborhood children as friends for fear of my safety. Also, while it was true that my father used to travel frequently to buy merchandise for the store, I had never been away from both parents for any length of time. I was overjoyed when, at least once a month, my father came to Cologne on Friday to bring me home for the weekend. I loved the Friday night kiddush (the Hebrew blessing over wine that helps mark the start of the Sabbath) as well as the fatherly blessing when he would place his hands on my head and, in Hebrew, say the words, "May the Lord bless you and keep you." The Baum home was just as festive, and their family just as warm and devoted. But it wasn't home.

So, of course, when my father drove me back to Cologne on Sunday nights, I made it as difficult as possible for him to leave. With tears running down my cheeks, I would wail the same tune each time: "Even though the Baums are so nice, they still are not my Papa and my Mama." Every time, he had to physically tear himself away from me to put the goodbyes to an end. But I would always calm down right after he left. Spoiled as I was, I frequently made life miserable for the Baums. But it really was a good deal for me. With their daughter Margot and son Heinz around, for the first time, I finally had two friends with whom to play. We walked to school together every day and enjoyed one another's company.

Our school was known as the Jawne (pronounced yav-neh), directed by a man named Dr. Erich Klibansky. It comprised a number of buildings inside a small compound, including its own synagogue. According to a book by a former Cologne rabbi, Adolf Kober, during 1936–37, the number of students was 410, having grown from 178 just six years earlier. The teachers were excellent. Unfortunately, my abilities as a student were not. But with remedial help from the school, supervision from the Baums, and some extra help from their kids, I managed to squeeze by. I remained at the Jawne until November 1938, when my world and that of my family was shattered, setting off a chain of events that changed our lives forever.

CHAPTER 2

Kristallnacht and Sachsenhausen

As I headed out for my walk to school on the morning of November 10, 1938, exactly a week after my twelfth birthday, I did not realize I had seen the inside of a classroom in Germany for the last time. Nazi terror was about to leave my childhood innocence strewn in the ashes and rubble enveloping Cologne's Jewish neighborhoods, although it would take many weeks and months for me to comprehend the reality of the situation.

Already, throughout the night of November 9–10 in Cologne, Nazi storm troopers had been pulling Jewish men out of their houses and marching them through the streets. Under encouragement by the "brownshirts," residents pelted Jews with potatoes, tomatoes, and other garbage, kicking and humiliating them. I slept through the uproar that took place during the night because it occurred far from the house. Then I was further spared the sight of this violence because our route to school followed smaller streets, not main thoroughfares.

But I would see more than enough on my walk to the Jawne with Cantor Baum's children, Margot and Heinz. As we approached the Roonstrasse synagogue, smoke filled our nostrils and fire caught our eyes. The beautiful synagogue, which dated to 1899, was engulfed in flames. Nazis had scattered the synagogue's Torahs, which are the sacred scrolls containing the laws and teachings of Judaism, as well as dozens of prayer books and tallitot (prayer shawls), setting them ablaze on the street. The fire department was there with pumper trucks, accompanied by police. But nobody was pouring water on the fire, let alone preparing hoses. All simply stood around and took in the scene, watching to ensure the flames did not spread to Aryan buildings. Next, we passed the Glockengasse synagogue, where Baum was cantor. That landmark building was built in 1861 in the Moorish style. It, too, was being destroyed by flames.

As we arrived at the Jawne, we witnessed a similar scene. To my eyes, it looked as if all of the buildings in the compound were in flames. I later found out that only the synagogue attached to the school, Adath Jeshurun, burned that night, although the school, too, was destroyed by bombs by the end of World War II.

I was unable to understand what was unfolding because of how my parents protected me from the reality of Nazi persecutions. Of course, I was aware to some extent of these persecutions, but my father taught me that there were still many good people, even among the Nazis, so I never assumed the worst. Let's be honest—at some point, most children fantasize about their school burning down so they can get out of attending classes. That's exactly what came to my mind. I thought it was great—no school today, and none for the next few weeks. I wasn't the only one. Other classmates were cheering, too.

I am sure Margot, Heinz, and I would have asked Cantor Baum to explain what was happening after we returned home to Jülicher Strasse No. 19. But as we arrived, more horror ensued. My heart cries now for Margot and Heinz as I think about the scene, though again it did not fully sink in at the time. The whirl of events had me in a daze. A half-dozen storm troopers had grabbed Cantor Baum and his wife by the arm and by the scruffs of their neck and were dragging them downstairs to the front door. Margot and Heinz were screaming, "Mama! Papa!" The storm troopers paid no attention. Their parents were speechless and powerless to resist. Within a few moments, Cantor Baum and his wife had been shoved into a truck and were gone, while a few storm troopers remained behind to toss the Baums' furniture out the windows and into the street. I assumed the cantor and his wife might be away for a while and then return. I didn't realize that they were being taken to a railroad station for deportation to Poland. There was no way to imagine what awaited them—the concentration camps.

All I knew is that we were alone in the house without any adults. We were confused and frightened. None of us knew what to do. Finally, I went upstairs, picked up the telephone, and called my mother.

"The cantor and his wife just got taken away," I said. "We're all by ourselves."

"Don't worry. I'm sending (a driver with) our car to take you home," my mother said. She made it clear to me that she, at least, understood what was going on. But how could she understand so clearly? What did she know that I did not? She did mention that my father wasn't home, but she didn't say it in a way that seemed unusual. Little did I know how truly alarming it was.

CR

Before November 7, 1938, no one knew the name of a 17-year-old Polish Jew named Herschel Grynszpan. However, his actions that day marked the beginning of a series of events that changed not only my life but that of every Jew in Germany. Grynszpan, a teenager just five years older than I, was living in Paris when the Nazis decided to arrest and deport all German Jews of Polish origin. Because Poland wanted no part of them, either, they were left stranded in a small town along the German-Polish border. Grynszpan was enraged when he received a postcard from his father informing him that his family members were among the 12,000 Polish Jews trapped in this nightmare.

Grynszpan reacted in a way his father never could have foreseen. He walked into the German Embassy in Paris, said he was a German resident, and requested to see an embassy official. The clerk on duty asked an embassy diplomat, Ernst vom Rath, to speak to him. Grynszpan walked into vom Rath's office, pulled out a revolver, and shot him five times. Vom Rath died two days later.

This was an act that any respectable, civilized human being would condemn, regardless of the outrages being committed by the German government against the Jews. But the Nazis, not satisfied simply to remove Jews from the nation's economic machinery, used the assassination as an excuse to proceed with the next step toward resolving the Jewish "problem." They orchestrated a pogrom on the night of November 9–10, setting out to arrest all Jewish males from the ages of 14 to 83, with the goal of accelerating the widespread Jewish emigration already underway.

This would become known as Kristallnacht, the "Night of Broken Glass." Besides conducting arrests, members of Hitler's SA (*Sturmabteilung*) and SS (*Schutzstaffel*) beat Jewish men and women into a bloody mess, plundering their businesses, breaking their windows, and destroying everything in sight. They did not stop there. The Nazis burned or destroyed 267 synagogues and 7,500 Jewish businesses, and killed at least 91 Jews, according to the United States Holocaust Memorial Museum. The insanity stood in contrast to the old German saying, "*Am Deutschen Wesen, Soll Die Welt Genesen*" (The world will benefit from the German character and conduct).

Little did I realize that the insanity had already arrived at our front door in Lüdenscheid. I would only learn the details years later through conversations with my parents and reading my father's diary.

☙

Hours before my fateful walk through Cologne on November 10, at 6 a.m., there was a knock at my family's house at Paulinenstrasse No. 10.

My mother opened the door and a police officer, accompanied by four or five others, asked for my father.

"Is your name *der Jude* (the Jew) Herman Behrend?" the officer asked as my father came to the door.

"*Ja*, Herman Behrend," he replied.

Both my mother and father were at the door at that point. They watched as the policemen loaded their pistols, pointed them, and told him he was under arrest. My mother began to scream.

"What's the matter with you?" the officer asked my mother sarcastically. "(You are screaming) just because we are coming with guns?" Then, he turned to my father and said, "We would be happy to use them if you intend to take flight."

Members of the police contingent then brushed past my parents and stormed through our house looking for Lea Ripp, a Polish Jew's wife staying with my family. My parents had taken in Mrs. Ripp and her newborn son Uriel a week earlier, after the Germans had arrested her husband Julius and deported him. At the moment, she was still confined to bed with the baby, now two weeks old.

As my mother calmed down, she was speechless. She could only bring herself to groan, "I'm getting very sick."

"You're getting sick because we are here?" the officer responded, his voice dripping with the same sarcasm.

As she regained composure, my mother pleaded with the police to leave Mrs. Ripp alone, saying she could not leave bed yet. They agreed to do so, but only until she was well enough to be moved. Sure enough, they returned a couple weeks later to send her and the baby to a concentration camp. My parents never heard from the Ripps again, leaving the young family's fate shrouded in mystery until, by chance, I came upon the name of Norbert Ripp, Lea's brother, in a 2011 issue of the *Jewish Exponent* (Philadelphia). I contacted Norbert and discovered that the family did not survive. The baby, Uriel, had been hidden in Brussels, Belgium, in hopes that he might make it through the war. But Uriel died in 1944 during an Allied air raid.

As for my father, there was little he could do except for one final act of defiance. He grabbed his half-dozen military medals and put them on, hoping the police would feel shame and recognize they were arresting not some faceless Jew but a decorated World War I veteran. On November 9, 1934, exactly four years before the onset of the overnight Kristallnacht terror, Germany had presented one of those medals "in the name of the Führer and Chancellor of the Reich." Now, with that very Cross of Honor draped across his chest, he emptied his pockets as police took him into custody to become a prisoner of Hitler's Reich.

❧

As they had done in Cologne, Hannover, Berlin, and throughout Germany, the SA and the SS had gone on a rampage in Lüdenscheid. The Nazis described the events of the night as a "spontaneous" outpouring of rage and anger against the Jews. But the truth was, it had been conducted "in the name of the Führer," orchestrated from the beginning by Hitler's henchman, Goebbels. In Lüdenscheid, in fact, subsequent accounts showed that the citizenry was rather restrained, with few local residents joining the storm troopers in the smashing and looting.

On the morning of November 10, while my father was being arrested, two clothing stores were looted and destroyed—those owned by Julius Ripp and a man named Oscar Cahn. The loot was tossed onto the street and set on fire. Because my father's store had closed a couple months earlier, it was left alone. There was no synagogue in Lüdenscheid for them to destroy. Until 1936, our congregation had met in a prayer room on the upper floor of a restaurant, and then it moved to the city library until the synagogue finally closed.

As for my father, he was taken to the police station, where he was forced to surrender his hat, suspenders, and any remaining items in his possession. The police placed him into so-called protective custody in the prison basement of the town hall. He shared a cell with Cahn and another man from nearby Altena.

On the first day, the local officials treated him decently. With the consent of the local police chief, my mother was able to speak to my father and bring warm clothing. It's no surprise that the local police, who knew my father and his contributions to the community, treated him well. At one point, a girl brought him a substantial portion of food, but he refused to eat it. It turned out the girl was the police chief's daughter, leaving the chief puzzled why my father wouldn't accept the plate.

He said, "Herman, what is the matter with you? Why don't you eat the food? I'm not giving you the regular prison food. This food comes off my table. It's the same stuff that I ate tonight also. Why won't you eat it?" But my father still said no. He didn't want special treatment while fellow Jewish prisoners went hungry.

Later that night, the chief returned to my father's cell. This time, the chief placed himself at risk. He tried to help my father escape.

"Behrend," the chief implored, "get the hell out of here as fast as you can. Go to Switzerland. Leave. Because once you are in the hands of the gestapo, when they pick you up, I cannot help you anymore. Your cell door is open. Go, leave, take off."

My father thanked him, but again, the answer was no. My father feared the gestapo would retaliate against the other prisoners if he disappeared. He was also braver than he should have been because he still believed his wartime service would shield him from any harsh treatment. He refused to believe otherwise.

The next day, more Jewish prisoners arrived at the Lüdenscheid jail from nearby towns. Altogether, about 50 Jews were now in custody. Soon, the gestapo arrived and the humane treatment ended. The first thing the gestapo commissioner told the prisoners was that they were headed on a "journey to nowhere."

"There's nothing for you to talk about," he barked. "Instead, you should think about the name Grynszpan." The words sent a chill through my father.

First, the gestapo took them to the court prison in Dortmund, where some 800 Jews were being held, and where the gestapo relieved him of his finest watch. The next morning, which was the Sabbath, a joint force of gestapo and local police paraded the group of prisoners through the city as if these innocent Jews were dangerous, hardened criminals. My father and the others were forced to hold signs high above their heads with such inscriptions as, "We are the murderers of Rath," "We are the traitors of our country," and "We dirty Jews are to blame for all our misfortunes." Finally, upon reaching the railroad station in Dortmund, my father received a slice of dry bread to eat.

The prisoners were convinced they were headed for a concentration camp. But where? The train passed through Hannover, and as they approached Berlin, they realized the answer: Concentration Camp Sachsenhausen, in Oranienburg, 22 miles north of the capital.

The journey continued onward, and at 5 p.m. they reached Berlin and briefly stopped. Again, the train began to move. Traveling through the deep dark night, my father increasingly began to dread what lay ahead in the camp. As it neared this destination, the train crept along, slowly, in a sinister way. Suddenly, it jolted to a stop. The doors were pulled open. A pack of thugs in SS uniforms stormed into the rail cars.

"You murderous pack of Jews! You dirty pigs! You heaps of shit! Why aren't you outside?!" the storm troopers yelled, brandishing clubs and truncheons.

Then they descended upon the prisoners, striking them repeatedly over the head, neck, and shoulders. One after another, my father and fellow prisoners collapsed to the ground in front of the train, only to continue to be kicked and beaten mercilessly. My father was in disbelief and felt as if he were in a trance. Emerging from the trance, he saw only mounted bayonets and blinding lanterns. The cries for help from fellow prisoners unnerved him. Finally, the light revealed what had happened. Dead and wounded Jews were lying everywhere.

In quick steps, they were now forced to run through difficult, heavily wooded terrain in the dark of night. The men in SS uniforms yelled, leaving the prisoners in fear of being clubbed to death at any moment. Some could suffer the horror no longer, committing suicide by cutting their wrists. Others suffered heart attacks and collapsed. Nothing in my father's service to the Kaiser in World War I compared with the terror he endured on this night march. Even the unbelieving Jews began to pray. The sounds of *Shema Yisrael*, the affirmation of the Jewish faith, could be heard through the night as they begged God for deliverance. After what seemed an eternity but was really only a half hour, the prisoners arrived at the gates of Sachsenhausen. We now know they were among 6,000 Jews taken there in the aftermath of Kristallnacht, with the remainder of the 30,000 arrested sent to Buchenwald and Dachau.

Roll call took place at 7 p.m. Everyone's personal information was taken down. Then, the guards forced my father and his fellow prisoners to stay on their feet until 4 the following afternoon—a full 21 hours without food or rest. My father was in a state of exhaustion he had never experienced before. All they received was a quarter cup of undrinkable water handed out by fellow prisoners. Once 4 p.m. arrived, they were permitted to bathe. Their heads were shorn bald. Then they were given new clothing: a thin-striped prison suit, one shirt, a pair of socks, and a towel. Finally, a group of 450 Jews was led to a barrack designed to be occupied by 75 persons, and they were given food. My father could not discern the consistency of the food, but it was edible. In fact, in these prewar days, before concentration camps gave way to extermination camps, they were able to receive food that had taste and satisfied hunger. All in all, considering the circumstances, he felt he could not complain about that one aspect.

He considered the foremen guarding the Jewish prisoners to be relatively humane despite being seasoned criminals who had been sentenced to serve time in the camps. They were like precious pearls compared to Hitler's SS hordes. They saw themselves in the prisoners, thinking of the suffering that they had endured themselves, and showed empathy and a bit of respect. The treatment changed whenever the SS guards appeared. Then, the foremen would copy their masters.

On the following night, my father and the other inmates finally would get a chance to sleep. They had to be in bed at 7 p.m. My father shivered throughout the night with only two thin blankets for protection from the cold as he lay on the floor. But before being told to go to bed, the men were informed that doctors, sick bays, and hospital care were reserved for Germans and not "dirty Jews." The only place for Jews, the Germans said, was work and a coffin.

At 4:30 a.m., the guards swept into the barrack and began screaming orders, pushing, shoving, and kicking my father and the others. Roll call was at 6:15 a.m., followed by assignments to work details. Periodically, groups were called aside to receive punishment for nonexistent infractions. Starting at 8 a.m. each day, guards forced my father to perform such work as shoveling sand, carrying rocks, and toting 40-pound sacks of cement. He was grateful to be among the group selected by the foremen for those jobs and not for the work detail outside the camp. The SS beat and humiliated prisoners, with full approval of Sachsenhausen's commandant, who not only applauded his guards but also rewarded them with decorations and promotions. Lunchtime was 11:30 a.m. My father's stomach gnawed with hunger as he chewed on the single dry piece of bread that served as a ration. Those with cigarettes were allowed to smoke.

Labor continued until 4 p.m., when they marched to the main section of camp for the ordeal of evening roll call. New arrivals had to find their correct places, which was impossible amid the confusion, and resulted in many being beaten and kicked. It would usually take until 6 p.m. until everyone found their correct spots among the thousands of prisoners, by which time the exhaustion was extreme. Most of the time, my father found himself drenched to the skin. He froze, shivered, and shook like a dog because they had been exposed to the cold all day without being permitted to sit. All the coughing, sneezing, and nose blowing made it difficult for him to hear what the guards were saying. If the prisoners were fortunate enough to actually be dismissed by 6 p.m., he blessed his good luck. Most times, they were not.

Instead, the guards forced them to sing two or three songs, repeating what they were forced to sing earlier during roll call. These songs were required to demonstrate to the surrounding communities how "happy" the inmates were in their surroundings. The prisoners were forced to continue standing and exercising until they were ordered to bed, sometimes without being fed. When things went well, they would assemble in front of the barracks to pick up their meals. My father felt more like an animal than a man as he joined the others in lunging at the bowls of food as if they were starving lions. He had to watch not to step on those who were crawling because they hadn't the strength to walk. After the meal came singing lessons, and at 7:30, it was lights out and time for bed.

Each morning, prisoners were assigned to remove and dispose of comrades who were too sick to work. As the Germans had promised, many found the coffin. In my father's barrack, five to eight Jews were dying every day.

The deaths slowed after the first eight days. Prisoners' treatment improved, but only slightly. Morning and night, my father could not shake the deep chill pervading his body. The hours standing in the rain, snow, wind, and icy cold were unbearable. And no heat could be used in the barracks. He was not even permitted to relieve himself. No prisoners were allowed to use the toilets from 7 in the morning to 6 at night.

The SS continued to mete out punishments for any infractions as if back in the Middle Ages. They tied the hands of offenders behind their backs, hoisted them up, tied them to a pole, and left them hanging for five to ten hours. Others were tied and strapped to a rack, then clubbed with a wooden stick on their naked buttocks between 15 and 25 times. I don't know whether my father was subjected to these punishments—he never discussed it in later years. But the language in his diary gives a hint. It talks about "hands being tied behind your back" while being hung on a pole, while "others" were strapped to a rack. I take that to mean he was probably among those left dangling in the air. Of one thing it is clear. My father feared he would die.

◌◌

On November 10, I stayed in the Baums' house in Cologne with the two other children all day, waiting for a car to arrive. The wait dragged through the rest of the morning, then into the afternoon. We were still alone as night fell.

But then arrived our Wanderer, a sporty, black luxury car with a roll-down top, manufactured in Germany until the end of World War II. We had several employees in our beautiful household on Paulinenstrasse along with a store employee who also served as chauffeur. But the chauffeur and the other household employees would not make the drive. They feared being arrested if spotted giving a ride to a Jew and figured the odds were against them in such a distinctive car. We had one employee from my parents' former store, however, who was tiny in size but had a heart as big as they come and was as anti-Nazi as possible. He was willing to take the risk. After nightfall, so we wouldn't be seen, he made the drive to Cologne and brought me home.

Sadly, we had to leave Margot and Heinz Baum, my first and only child-hood friends, alone in the house at 19 Jülicher Strasse. As the years passed, I would often think about them, wondering if they died or survived the war. It would be some 25 or 30 years later before I learned their fate.

I don't recall what my mother told me about my father's whereabouts when we arrived home, but I'm certain she mentioned nothing about a concentration camp. Given what was happening with my father, however, she had already de-cided to get me out of Lüdenscheid. She contacted my father's sister Margarete, or Aunt Grete as I called her, and asked if she could give me shelter in her home in Hannover. Aunt Grete agreed without hesitation, and I was driven off to stay with my aunt, who was a live-in nurse specializing in taking care of patients suf-fering from mental and neurological disorders. She was taking care of a wealthy Jew named *Kommerzienrat* Richard Molling (Kommerzienrat is an honorary title given to a distinguished businessman). His mind was so far gone because of what we probably today would call advanced Alzheimer's disease that the Ger-mans were leaving them both alone for the time being. Before I left Lüdenscheid for Hannover, I saw the fear and disbelief on the face of my mother and our household staff. I began to feel unsettled and nervous, but I couldn't understand what was going on.

Aunt Grete did not say much about my father's or my family's situation, either. I was accustomed to my father traveling to other cities to buy merchandise for the store, so I wasn't worried enough to ask many questions. I did finally learn around this time, however, that my father had been taken to the police station. I may not have understood the seriousness of the situation, but I finally knew true anxiety and fear for the first time of my life. I never knew what each day would bring, and I knew that life as I had known it would never be the same. It was like a child's view of a thunderstorm. You see the lightning, but you can't understand it.

At some point shortly after my father's arrest, my mother discovered through the police chief in Lüdenscheid what it would take to get my papa's re-lease. The Nazis wanted a guarantee that we would leave Germany as soon as possible and never return. My mother began working tirelessly to meet their edict. Then, after 14 days in Sachsenhausen, another small ray of light was al-lowed to shine. Prisoners were permitted to send their first postcard home, let-ting families know where they were.

രെ

Shortly before Kristallnacht, my parents and other members of my family on my mother's side began to realize the gravity of the situation facing Germany's Jews. Although they could not anticipate the true urgency, they saw the need to flee before the noose grew so tight that it would be too late. All settled on the United States as a destination, as far away from Germany as possible.

But it would be a difficult proposition. Under its quota system, the United States had only limited spots available for German immigrants, and an affidavit was required to obtain a quota number. The affidavit was designed to prevent immigrants from posing a financial burden to their newly adopted nation. The process meant finding sponsors in the United States willing to sign a sworn guarantee to support the immigrants if necessary and, through disclosure of tax returns and other documents, to prove they had the necessary financial resources. My parents called everywhere, trying to find even a long-lost relative who could help, and eventually did succeed in finding one to sign the affidavit. But when US immigration officials reviewed the documents, they ruled that the relative lacked sufficient means and denied us a quota number.

But there was another way to increase the odds of having your affidavit accepted—placing a large fund in an American bank to be available for the immigrants' use upon arrival. Those of us seeking to flee no longer had any significant amount of money available.

But one family member did. One of my mother's two brothers, Otto Oppenheim, had accumulated considerable wealth since moving from Germany to Denmark about a decade earlier. Otto, who was married to my Aunt Irene and had three children, had ascended to director for Scandinavian countries for Louis Dreyfus and Company, a French international grain-shipping firm, and was living in Copenhagen. Realizing Otto was our only hope, my parents and other family members placed desperate phone calls to him in Denmark.

In 2010, speaking on *Yom Hashoah* (Holocaust Remembrance Day) in front of her synagogue in New York City, one of those three children, my late cousin Hanna, spoke about those phone calls. She recalled that her father at first was unsure what to do. He was concerned about his own children's fate and had set the money aside for them in case they might need it someday. Her mother Irene did not hesitate. "You must help them," she said to her husband.

In all, 11 members, from four different families would seek to emigrate from Germany to the United States. In addition to the three members of my immediate family, there were the families of my mother's other brother, Hugo Oppenheim, and Aunt Irene's brother, Felix Schwarz, as well as one of my cousins, Fred Jellin. Uncle Otto provided $7,500 per family, or $30,000 to the City Bank of New York as a deposit to demonstrate our living expenses would be covered upon arrival in the United States.

But months later, as we were rushing to flee, we also found we needed money to survive in Cuba because we couldn't go directly to America. A Louis Dreyfus and Company affiliate subsequently deposited $6,000 in the National City Bank of Havana for the families to be able to emigrate there temporarily. The combined $36,000 was the equivalent of about $600,000 today.

"I hope that they (the Nazis) will honor their pledge for Herman's freedom and release," Uncle Otto wrote in a November 18 telegram to my mother in which he detailed the Cuban deposit.

However, as anything of value was being confiscated, my mother wrote to Otto one more time to ask if he could provide more money for living expenses in Cuba. Sadly, he wrote back that the money he had given us in order to save our lives was completely exhausted. He had nothing left.

In mid-1938, because of Uncle Otto's help, my parents had been able to travel to Stuttgart and obtain our quota number at the US embassy. But we would have to wait for our number to come up.

After Kristallnacht, my mother informed Uncle Otto that we needed a guarantee of our departure to save my father, and he continued with every ounce of energy at his disposal. He applied for visas anywhere that would consider accepting Jews—places like Chile, Argentina, Brazil, and Cuba—until our turn to come to America might arrive.

Finally, his efforts paid off. I don't know how much it cost, but my uncle still had enough left to pay a large sum to a business associate, who suddenly was able to grease the right palms so we could obtain visas and landing permits that would permit us to immigrate to the small island nation of Cuba, just 90 miles south of Florida. The landing permits should not have even been necessary. They were an added layer of bureaucracy that were essentially a legal bribe paid to corrupt Cuban officials.

My mother took the paperwork to the Nazis. She finally had the guarantee of our speedy departure that the Nazis were demanding in return for my father's freedom.

☙

The days were blending together in Sachsenhausen as November dragged to an end. My father was managing to survive the cold with only the thinnest of clothing, not even something to cover his head.

Early on a Friday morning, December 2, a group of orderlies burst into the barrack as everyone was still sound asleep. In loud voices, they read the names of 21 individuals who were to be released immediately. Among the names, he heard the words "Herman Behrend."

My father could not even trust his ears after 22 days of suffering and wondering if he would ever see the outside world again. Perhaps ten times he asked other prisoners if he had heard right, that his release from this hell was at hand. After a moment, he felt as if he had lost his senses. He began crying profusely and couldn't stop, collapsing to the ground. He couldn't understand what was happening. Finally, the flood of emotion slowed down and he regained his composure. Someone picked him up and sat him down.

He was given a haircut and a shave. Then he gave away every single belonging that he had with him, regardless of whether it was originally his. It was as if he wanted no connection to anything that had been part of this place. At the same time, he could not believe his sudden good fortune. He looked into the eyes of the poor souls he was leaving behind and understood the blessing being bestowed upon him this day.

"On the day that I was taken to this (camp), I never imagined in my wildest dreams that I would ever see my dearest wife or blessed Fritz again," he wrote in his diary. "The good Lord, however, must have heard my daily prayers and kept me in health in both body and soul."

Just one more time, he stood straight through from six in the morning until 7 at night. He received no food of any kind, but at this point he didn't care.

At the moment of discharge, the camp commandant explained the policy of the Third Reich toward its Jews. Their release was not due to good behavior, he said. The only reason they were being released was on condition that they leave Germany as quickly as possible. "Germany does not want to see you or have any part of you anymore," the commandant said. To my father, this was his once-beloved country's ultimate disgrace.

Escorted by a sentry to the camp gate, the 21 prisoners watched the barrier being raised and rejoiced for the first time in their golden freedom.

CR

My father, Oscar Cahn, and Salomon Gobas of Lüdenscheid, along with the others, marched through the camp gate and into the night. They were lost and started inquiring how to reach Oranienburg Railway Station. Most of my father's comrades didn't have a single Deutschemark on them. Fortunately, the Germans had returned to my father the 118 marks that they had confiscated upon his arrival at Sachsenhausen. With this money, he thought he could satisfy his hunger and those of his comrades. But nobody was inclined to help a bunch of Jews, especially ones with shaved heads and tattered suits and hats. They went into stores on both sides of the street to buy food. In each store, the response was, "We don't sell to dirty Jews." However, he was able to purchase train tickets. They boarded with empty stomachs and hunger pains to head to Berlin for the first leg of their journey home.

Even then, fear was their companion. Once seated in the train compartment at Oranienburg, they encountered an SS man from the concentration camp who also was en route to Berlin. His cruelty was unabated even outside the barbed-wire fence. He took one look at them and screamed, "Get up, you bunch of pigs. What kind of nerve do you Jew bastards have to seat yourselves on chairs which will later be used to seat Aryans?" Others on the train looked on in bewilderment. My father and the other former prisoners were still too timid after their incarceration, and too happy to be headed home, to say anything back. So they got up and, for the rest of the trip, stood at the windows in the walkway as one final epilogue to their imprisonment in Concentration Camp Sachsenhausen.

Upon arrival in Berlin, several men contacted their former business suppliers and pleaded with them to bring money so the released men could continue their journey home. Soon, there was practically more money than everyone could use. At the Berlin train station, the men entered a waiting room, slunk into a distant corner as if criminals on the run, and, this time, were served when they ordered heaping mounds of food. They fell upon the food like a pack of wolves, though nothing seemed to ease their hunger.

In Berlin, my father realized that he had no idea where my mother and I were. In the months before Kristallnacht, once our families had decided to leave Germany, my parents had decided not to renew the lease in Lüdenscheid. They signed a new one for an apartment in Cologne, where I could live with them and attend the Jawne school until whenever the time came to emigrate. Though there would be overlap between the end of one lease and the beginning of the other, the Cologne apartment would be ours as of December 1, 1938. However, this was December 2, and the Cologne lease would have been canceled by now as well, especially given the complications of renting to Jews anymore. His first thought was to call his sister, my Aunt Grete, in Hannover.

To him, the call took an eternity to go through. As he waited, he began to realize he did not know what he would say when Grete answered. So when she did, he was momentarily tongue-tied. She kept repeating, "*Hier ist Behrend bei Molling, hier ist Behrend bei Molling.*" (Here is Behrend at the house of Molling, here is Behrend at the house of Molling.)

Finally, the words gushed out, as if from a geyser. "*Hier ist Herman. Ich bin wieder auf freien Fusse.*" (Here is Herman, I am a free man again.)

Grete was so excited she could not respond at first. Finally, when she calmed down, my father asked if he could stay with her overnight and if someone could drive over and pick him up when the train was scheduled to arrive at the Hannover station. The D train left the Berlin Hauptbahnhoff Friedrichstrasse punctually at 10:00 p.m., with Kahn and Gobas from Lüdenscheid and several others aboard. In Berlin, they had bought Skat cards (Skat is the national card game of Germany), but none of the released prisoners were able to look at the cards or even touch them. Throughout the ride, my father stood in the aisle, staring out the window at a world where he would again be free. The train arrived in Hannover at 1:30 in the morning.

When he stepped off the train, Grete was standing on the platform. Not a word crossed their lips. Without a sound, they walked up to the car. They entered it, and slowly the driver began to pull away from the station. When they arrived at the Molling apartment, they went inside to a spread of coffee, rolls, and other light food. After three weeks in the concentration camp, he could no longer do what would be reflexive to anyone else—pour coffee into a mug, take a roll, and then sit and eat. Instead, his reaction was to take stock with his eyes to see if there was enough for him. He was fearful someone else would take his share.

It was only then that my father and Aunt Grete threw themselves into each other's arms and held each other tight. The relief at being reunited after weeks of wondering whether he would ever be seen alive again overwhelmed them. They barely spoke 20 words to each other that night as it slowly sunk in that the nightmare of my father's imprisonment was over.

Finally, after filling his stomach, he was ready to lie down. But he was caught by surprise as he walked in the bedroom to find me in the bed, fast asleep. As excited as he was to see me there, he just let me sleep in peace. My father remembered that the clock struck 3 a.m. as he drifted off into a deep sleep.

He was still asleep when I awoke in the morning. Oh, it was such a thrill to see him there! Perhaps he had let me sleep, but there isn't a 12-year-old in the world who would have done the same in return after being apart for so long. With a loud yell, I jumped on top of him. I cried and gave him a kiss. He wrapped me in a big embrace. I was overjoyed to feel safe in his arms again. His haggard appearance was frightening, but somehow he was able to ease my worries.

That night, Aunt Grete had gotten ahold of my mother Else to tell her that my father was free. But when he awoke, he could not wait any longer to talk to my mother and go see her. His call that day to Lüdenscheid was quickly connected, and it was then that he found out that my mother was out of our luxurious house and living in an unheated room on the ground floor of a family friend's home. They agreed to meet the following day and discuss the family's future. However, one thing was clear to both of them from their brief phone call. We could no longer live in Lüdenscheid. The best place for us until finalizing our departure from Germany would be in Hannover.

First my father needed to replace his ruined clothes. It took a few phone calls, but Aunt Grete was able to acquire all the necessary items from a Dr. Herzberg in Hannover.

My parents had agreed that my father would be picked up by car at Hagen Railroad Station to be taken to Lüdenscheid. But just as with my journey home from Cologne, the mere use of a car by a Jew was fraught with peril. On December 3, the Nazis enacted a decree banning Jews from owning or driving a car. Suddenly, my father's beautiful Wanderer was no longer his. After considerable effort, my mother devised a way to get him home. She approached an old family friend, who agreed to use his own car and take a chance by picking up my father and driving her as well. My mother had to go to the outskirts of Lüdenscheid in order to board the car before proceeding to the rail station, as the risk of being seen with a Jew in the car was too great. My mother awaited my father's arrival on the platform. The friend loaded them into the car for the return trip as if transporting criminals trying to escape across the border. Away they went to Lüdenscheid, where they disembarked at the same point along the city outskirts, walking the rest of the way to our house.

Here, my father could see how furiously my mother had been working since his arrest and why she was no longer living in our house. She had hired an international furniture moving company, A. W. Neukirch, which sent workers and moving vans to Lüdenscheid to pack up our family's belongings. A wooden container, called a lift, had to be built for shipping our things to our new home abroad. The container was so large it took up the entire width of the street.

My parents decided to sleep in our house one final time before bidding it farewell. My father was mired in daze and confusion, watching the workers pack up our things, not knowing how to respond as they asked whether items were bound for Cuba or the United States. He could only wonder to himself: Do I really have to leave my home, my country, my native land? Is there really no place for me, my wife, and my son to stay, to continue to live in peace? But clearly, as if there had previously been any doubt that our family would have to abandon Germany after laying down roots spanning at least four centuries, it was all now erased. No Jew could remain in Germany and live in safety.

We had always opened our doors to those in need in Lüdenscheid and for the Jews of our town. My parents could only fervently hope that during our exodus from Germany, we would be met with a bit of the helpfulness and assistance we had gladly given through the years. The beloved, hospitable House of Behrend was closing its gates forever. As for me, I never got to see the house again, although I did see the grounds of what was left of the compound upon visiting Germany with my wife Lisa nearly 25 years later.

As the realization of our fate crept in, my father's health began to deteriorate. He realized that he needed to return to Hannover and check himself into a hospital. Fortunately, the doctors' prescription for his recovery was simple: sleep, rest, peace and quiet, and lots to eat. He spent eight days in the hospital while my mother stayed in our friend's damp, dreary room, returning to the house by day to finish packing our belongings as best as she could.

With repression against Jews so high, my father and aunt discovered it was an arduous task to find a place where all three of us could stay in Hannover. They never located one. I remained with Aunt Grete, while my mother and father each wound up in separate rooms. Both of my parents' rooms were cold. They froze terribly. The only warmth was when they returned to the comfort of the Molling house. Because Richard Molling lived alone, with just Aunt Grete for company, he was glad to have us as visitors. He was particularly kind to me, and though his mind was often in a fog, I enjoyed his kindness and company. My parents were often there in time for afternoon coffee. Most of the time, they would stay with Aunt Grete for the evening meal, always, of course, providing food.

The situation for the Jews of Germany continued to deteriorate daily. In parks and public squares, Jews were allowed to sit only on specially designated benches. Barber shops refused to serve Jews. Movies and cafés were forbidden by law to allow Jews to enter. From the largest department stores to the smallest shops, signs stated, "Jews are not wanted here as customers." There were even doctors who refused to treat Jews; there was one female doctor in Hannover who was fired upon discovery that she had treated a Jewish mother who was unable to produce breast milk for her baby. The woman finally was able to obtain milk from an Aryan mother, but it was too late, and the baby died.

With the gestapo using a special division to conduct house searches and arrests in Jewish households, we knew we had to move as quickly as possible. But now, we were faced with new obstacles that threatened our departure, and time was running out.

CR

A new law now placed a "billion mark" penalty upon the Jews to pay for the damage for which they were supposedly responsible on Kristallnacht. Jews were to present itemized lists of belongings that they wished to take with them upon leaving the country. No person or piece of property could leave Germany without the authorities' approval, and anything of value was confiscated as the family's contribution toward the billion marks. My father had traveled to Münster three times to inquire on the status of these lists. Each time, the authorities conceived of every imaginable excuse for the delays, always promising that the approved lists of what we could take with us were on our way to us in Hannover.

In these final days, one or both of my parents made almost daily trips to Cologne, Hamburg, Bremen, Münster, and Lüdenscheid to try to straighten out the mess before it was too late. As of February 22, 1939, with our ship's scheduled departure just three days away, we had yet to receive our lists. Our anxiety mounted.

With time running short, my father headed for Münster on February 23 in one last-ditch effort to get the necessary documents before the deadline. Upon his arrival on Münster, he learned that we had been victims of another stroke of antisemitism. The approved lists had been issued a long time ago, but no one had wanted to bother to forward them to us. For the privilege of being allowed to take our old furniture, linens, and other various items, we were required to pay 3,005 marks to a bank in Berlin. Meanwhile, we discovered which of our possessions were being confiscated. The Nazis were seizing nearly all of our silver, including religious items such as Sabbath candlesticks, kiddush wine cups, and our havdalah spice box, as well as other mundane items such as knives, forks, and spoons.

Gestapo inspectors went through everything we had packed in the lift. The process dragged on for the entire time up until our scheduled departure. Nothing could be placed back in the lift until the gestapo said so. I watched the gestapo officers open up every sheet and pillowcase to make sure nothing was hidden inside. They even had a specialist go through my father's stamp collection, ripping out any of value; I still have the remaining collection to this day. Of course, my toys and other possessions were gone, too. Only my trains and building set survived. They were placed in the lift, although we were in New York for a year before my parents were able to borrow enough money to get the items in the lift delivered to our apartment.

What could we do? As my father wrote in his diary, "We were forced into consenting to all chicanery, as our ship was leaving. We could not and would not remain in this country of thieves and robbers any longer, even if it meant that we would have to leave all our possessions behind."

Many antique items, fortunately, survived, including our Seder plate of 1710. The Nazis were too stupid to realize the value of these items because they were only made of pewter.

In the weeks before our ship was set to steam out of Hamburg, Uncle Otto had concocted a plan for us to prevent having our money and jewelry fall into Nazi hands. Freighters often had a few cabins for passengers, and Uncle Otto knew a steward for Louis Dreyfus and Company who worked to take care of passengers on such ships. The steward offered to take anything of value on one of the freighters crossing the Atlantic, depositing everything in a bank or safe in Argentina or some Latin American country, where we would claim the items later. We had no other choice, so we divested ourselves of everything of value and gave it to the steward.

I was so happy with this arrangement because my father had a beautiful watch on a gold chain that I loved. It was the kind you put on a buttonhole in a vest pocket. When you pressed it, it would chime the time with the most beautiful sound. I adored playing with it and hoped someday it would be mine.

Unfortunately, the steward's plan only worked for one person—the steward. We never saw him or any of our valuables again. The Nazis allowed émigrés to leave with 10 marks apiece, or the equivalent of $2.50, so that's all we had.

As a parting gift from the Nazis, they provided some more degradation—a name change. They had created a list of first names considered clearly identifiable as Jewish. Any Jew whose first name was not on the list was forced to add Israel (for a male) or Sara (for a female) as a middle name. So my passport read Fritz Bernhard Israel Behrend, with a big red "J" on it for *Jude*.

My father went on from Münster to Bremen, a large German port city. After our heartfelt farewell to Aunt Grete, my mother and I met him there on February 24, where we also met the family of my Uncle Hugo and Aunt Herta Oppenheim (their son, Gerd, was ill and would temporarily remain behind with my cousin Fred Jellin until being well enough to travel). The Schwarz family joined us at the point of our departure, Hamburg. For our final night in Germany, we stayed at the Hotel Reichshof, where a notice was issued stating that "guests of the Jewish race" were no longer permitted to eat in the dining room with the other guests. Then on Saturday afternoon, February 25, 1938, it was time to board a ship called the *Iberia*.

The indignities were not complete, however. At the last moment, we were not permitted to go on board. My mother was sent into one room with my female aunts and cousins, while my father and I were sent into another with the male relatives, where we were held for hours. We were strip searched, with Germans in white robes checking inside our mouths and our asses, as well as inside the women's and girls' private parts, to see if diamonds or other valuables were being smuggled outside the country. The Germans clearly seemed to enjoy subjecting us to this humiliation. The last thing taken was the wedding ring right off my mother's finger. I took things as in stride as possible because it was so bewildering, while I could see my father was fuming. My mother cried for hours afterward.

But the time was dragging on. Between being searched and waiting idly in these rooms, we were held for many hours. Our fear mounted that we might not get to board our ship. And who knew what would become of us if we couldn't leave with the *Iberia*?

Finally, we were permitted to board. Even then, we were afraid that the Germans would pull us off the boat for some other reason we could not even imagine. It was only when we steamed out of port that our fears were finally put to rest. At last, the nightmare was over. We were on our way to Havana.

CHAPTER 3

Biding Time in Cuba

It was only in those final weeks, as my father was running from city to city, from one German government office to another, to finalize our visas and exit paperwork, that it finally began to sink in that we were leaving the only country I had ever known. But my parents had yet to tell me.

Finally, one day, I pulled my father aside and asked, "Where are we going?"

After his years in the army, my father was skilled at giving out information the way he had received it in the military—on a need-to-know basis.

"We're going to Cuba," he said.

He figured that was sufficient explanation for a 12-year-old and made it clear the conversation was over, at least in his eyes. However, I had to have more if my curiosity was to be satisfied. If he had said China or Canada, at least I would have a familiar-sounding place to point to on a map. But Cuba? I couldn't have even guessed which continent that was on.

"I've never heard of Cuba," I told him, persuading him to spend a few more moments on the topic.

He got right to the point. "Well," he asked, "you see me when I'm smoking cigars?"

"Yes," I replied.

"They come from Cuba."

So that was it. Cuba and cigars—what more could I possibly want to know? And I wasn't going to press him a second time.

I tried to pry information from my mother as well and tried to see if the decision to head for Cuba was irreversible, which, of course, it was. I asked whether we couldn't just go back to Lüdenscheid. But she said we couldn't because we had given up the house. My parents were still sheltering me from painful truths for as long as they could. I would have to be content knowing we couldn't go back, that we were going to some speck on the map I had never heard of before, and I was not to receive any real explanation of why we had to leave at all. I would have no choice but to let these little tidbits of information from my parents hold me for a while until we departed Hamburg. From that point on, we'd go from the chaos of trying to flee to finding ways to pass time during two-and-a-half weeks of ocean travel, then finding more ways to pass time for more than a year in Cuba as we waited and hoped our quota number would be called to let us immigrate to the United States.

CR

After the initial elation of steaming out of German waters, my mother and father were furious as we saw our accommodations aboard the *Iberia*. Uncle Otto had arranged for us to purchase first-class tickets, but we discovered at the dock that the Germans would not permit Jews to purchase first- or tourist-class tickets. We wound up in steerage along with Uncle Hugo's family from Rhaden and Aunt Irene's family from Berlin. Our cabins were below the waterline, crowded and with air so stuffy it was difficult to breathe. My father and I shared one cabin with five other passengers. The women were separated from the men, although they shared a cabin with similar accommodations. It was brutally cold when we went on board. We shivered to the point that we wondered when we would ever get rid of the chill.

As for my poor mother, things couldn't have been any worse, even though it would turn out that the food and service were of far better quality than the cabins we purchased. She got seasick before the ship ever left the dock. With tears running down her face, in a soulful voice, she pleaded with my father, "I want to go back to Lüdenscheid!" She was unable to eat. She remained in bed the first few days. My father finally got her a deck chair and brought her up on deck, where she stayed for the remainder of the trip. The only time she left that chair was to use the bathroom.

Although nothing except pulling up to the dock in Cuba would do anything to improve my mother's mood, for the rest of us, our moods were indeed brightening. As we pulled away from Hamburg into the North Sea, slowly, cautiously, we began to exhale in relief. Soon, as the shoreline drifted from sight, there was a sense of euphoria. Family members hugged. They kissed. They laughed and cried out in the kind of excited tones they probably hadn't used for months or even years under Nazi rule. We were leaving danger behind. We were heading from darkness to light, a place—wherever Cuba was—where we no longer had to fear for our lives. Although I only had a vague sense of the peril we had escaped, I did understand that we were embarking on a new adventure. I would begin to comprehend the extent of that danger gradually on the ship through conversations I overheard topside as people discussed the persecution they had endured.

I would begin to understand more fully in the weeks to come as we began our new life under the Caribbean sun.

Our ocean voyage included a few stops along the way, taking us to Antwerp, Belgium; Cherbourg, France; and the Portuguese capital of Lisbon before sailing to Cuba. In Antwerp we visited friends of Uncle Otto, a family named Feidheim. They showed us exceptional warmth and hospitality, serving us a beautiful entrée. In Lisbon, too, we were greeted by friends of Uncle Otto and Aunt Irene, a Professor Wohlwill and his wife. Here my father took me on a long car ride to explore the interior of Portugal. We visited various cloisters and castles in the province of Estremadura, engaging in the kind of excursions I would be fond of in my later years through Germany, other places in Europe, and beyond. At 6 p.m., the boat resumed its journey.

It had been brutally cold when we went aboard the *Iberia*. After eight days at sea, just past Lisbon, the warmth of the tropical sun set in. Swimming pools were erected on the decks. All our winter clothing was stowed away. For the next ten days, we saw only the sky and the water as the ship made its way across the Atlantic. My father and I enjoyed the trip thoroughly, never experiencing what my mother did.

Finally, on a sunny, hot, mid-March 1939 morning, our ship entered the harbor of Havana. Like Moses, with divine help, we had arrived at our promised land.

Unfortunately, for a while, we were too much like Moses. He never entered the promised land, and it started to appear we would not, either. After reviewing our entrance permits, Cuban officials told us that they had to conduct further checks on the documents' authenticity. We were then ferried to the island that the famous Morro Castle overlooks, guarding the entrance of Havana's harbor. We were taken to the official prison there, known as Tiscornia. Authorities took us to our bunks and issued blankets to spread over the bare rusty springs. Even my normally upbeat father began to despair.

"I left one concentration camp only to find myself in another," he groaned.

We would stay there for five days, but we soon discovered light amid the misery. We may have been "guests" in a converted prison, but here in Havana, there were Jews to greet us, though they spoke in a Spanish tongue that was strange to us. With some Yiddish, Hebrew, and hand signs, they made it clear we were welcome in this island nation.

One of our days at Tiscornia was a Saturday, the holy Jewish Sabbath. It was a day I will never forget. Little did we know that there was a group of local American women called the Menorah Sisterhood that had taken the refugees in Cuba under its wing. Apparently, the sisterhood had sent word to the Jewish community of Miami that another boatload of Jewish refugees was interned in Havana harbor. Overnight, an emergency charter flight was organized, and at noontime the next day, a large contingent of volunteers ferried across the harbor to start unloading equipment. A rabbi and female volunteers from a soup kitchen began toiling away in the sweltering heat to bring hospitality into our lives. They erected open tents to shield us from a merciless sun and brought stores of food, blankets, pillowcases, and clothing. You would never have known, as we later found out, that many of the ladies helping us were members of Miami's high society. When times were darkest, you really could count on members of your religion after all.

The most beautiful moment came when they ushered us to one of the open tents and the rabbi led a Sabbath service. Afterward, the women, who had set up tables and chairs for all, served us our first warm, kosher, and edible meal. They taught us the true meaning of the Sabbath.

The outpouring of warmth overwhelmed my mother. But the moment was bittersweet. She found herself crying and unable to compose herself. Back in Lüdenscheid, she was the one in high standing to whom members of the community looked. Now she was powerless and needy. She was the one who needed help, not the one providing it. She lost her appetite and wound up unable to eat the meal at all. This sense of loss was, in the most literal sense, the hardest pill for her to swallow. I, however, was not shy about making up for any food she could not consume.

After five days, Cuban authorities finally were satisfied with our documentation and allowed my family to leave detention at Tiscornia and stand free on Cuban soil. We thanked God for the abundance of his blessings. We wanted to find a synagogue to celebrate our first Sabbath and say prayers of gratitude. But this desire was about more than wishing to offer thanks. The one thing about being Jewish is, wherever you travel in the world, if you can find a synagogue, you can communicate. At the very least, you can read the same prayers in Hebrew, celebrate the same holidays, and perform the same rituals. Just as we had found a sense of kinship with the Jewish women of Miami, we now sought that sense of community in Havana itself, inquiring about a place to spend our first Friday night and celebrate our day of rest.

We succeeded in finding a synagogue. The congregations in Cuba that we found were of Portuguese descent, with temples built by Jews who must have settled in Cuba hundreds of years earlier. None of us spoke Portuguese or Spanish, Cuba's national language, so communication in the most basic sense was difficult. And the service varied from what we were accustomed to. Jews from Portugal and Spain are from a branch called Sephardic, while Jews of the rest of Europe are Ashkenazi. The dialects of Hebrew are slightly different, as are the rituals.

Even so, we were not disappointed. The service was familiar enough. The hymns and melodies were similar enough to the ones we knew that we could generally follow along. For the very first time, we felt at ease. We had found peace among strangers in a house of God far removed from our homes and loved ones. Oddly enough, I felt more at home in that Cuban shul than at many I have visited in later years in America. I sadly compare many of the places of worship today to the Tower of Babel because they change the chants and melodies frequently to suit their preferences. Many times I have felt like a stranger in America, my adopted homeland, because I could not keep up in the service and did not feel the same connection I did on that Sabbath in Cuba.

ᘉ

Just a couple of weeks after our arrival in Cuba, on April 3, Passover began, and we held our first Seder outside of Europe. Passover marked the exodus of the Jews from Egypt. This Passover marked our safe exodus from the land that my family had considered home for more than four centuries. We would again get a lesson on the warmth of our Jewish brethren. We had no idea how we could get matzo for the Seder, or whether it was even possible to obtain it in Cuba. We were discussing the situation at the butcher's shop when the proprietor interrupted us. He said he could help us because his family baked their own matzo. He told us to come back the next day and he would have some. We came back as he instructed, and sure enough, he had enough for our family. My father was grateful but was taken aback when the butcher refused to let him pay for it.

The butcher waved his hand. "I can't accept any money," he said. Then he thanked *us* for allowing him the mitzvah (good deed) of helping refugees who just escaped to this country and wanted to celebrate Passover.

"*Zissen Pesach*," he said, which means "have a sweet Passover."

Despite the butcher's priceless gesture, the Seder seemed like it would be a mournful beginning in a new world. We were far away from the home we knew and without many of the family and friends who had occupied their seats around the Seder table for as long as I could remember. We had little money for food. The Nazis had looted us of virtually all our valuables, including the silver vessels that had always adorned the table for this occasion, in exchange for allowing us to leave the fatherland, and our beloved Seder plate was in storage in New York with many of our other possessions. My heart felt weighted down by sadness. I remember the tears in my mother's eyes and the forlorn looks on the faces of the other participants at the table.

My father, however, would have none of this self-pity. Through his optimism and sheer force of will, he singlehandedly turned a dismal celebration into a deeply devotional event.

"Yes, I know that our ancestors brought with them their household goods and whatever wealth they possessed when God led Israel out of the land of Egypt," my father said. "But our exodus is more alike than different than that of Israel's from Pharaoh.

"With the young and the old, driving their cattle before them, they walked into the unknown giving praise to God for their deliverance. And what was the most precious of all things that they took on their long journey?" he asked, turning his gaze at each and every one of us at the table, although I know in retrospect he really was gazing most deeply at me.

"It was their children! They represented not only their future, but the future of all Israel. If we are sad, we have failed to be truly thankful for our abundant blessings. Like our ancestors, we here today are truly blessed and give praise to God for our deliverance."

ᑯ

My first impressions of Cuba in those initial weeks were that I had indeed entered a strange, exotic world. I had never seen a black person before. So I was utterly amazed when some neighborhood children came to play with me. I couldn't stop looking and comparing the dark skin on most of their bodies with the nearly white color on the palms of their hands and the bottoms of their feet. When I went home, I described to my father what I had seen and asked, "What is this?" He said, "I don't know."

They, in turn, clearly had no idea how to react to a young Jew from Germany. They were equally amazed by my clothing, speech, and manner. Though we couldn't speak a single word to one another, we still formed a bond, and I learned from them. I learned how to open a coconut, peel a mango, and how to tell a ripe fig from one that is not.

You cannot imagine how much these black-skinned, Spanish-speaking children meant to me. In Lüdenscheid, I had lived behind the walls of the Zeppelin compound without a single friend. In Cologne, with the exception of Cantor Baum's children Margot and Heinz, I was still a solitary, friendless boy. Now, regardless of whether we spoke the same language or not, regardless of whether we even had the same skin color, these were children my age. And they *played* with me. They were my first friends. I might not have understood the freedoms that the Nazis were taking away from us with the discriminatory laws targeting Jews, but here was a freedom I could understand. I was liberated from the walls that my parents had designed to protect me from the outside world but had also kept me from the most essential part of being a child—making friends and having fun.

We did not know where we would live when we landed at Havana. We just knew it would be arranged for us by an agency called Fernandez & Medina. In a telegram to my Aunt Herta in November 1938, Uncle Otto said a colleague from Louis Dreyfus and Company in Paris had referred the agency to him. "I am sure that they will be of help to you upon landing," he said. "I unfortunately do not know the gentlemen personally but am told that they are exceptionally worthy gentlemen."

The agency placed us in a one-floor house that was small but quite comfortable, very close to the harbor where we had landed. It was stucco and had three bedrooms, one of which I shared with my parents, and one bathroom. The house also had a courtyard and a large porch outside, where everyone would often sit to pass the time. My parents and I shared the house with Uncle Hugo and Aunt Herta and cousin Gerd, and later another cousin, Fred Jellin. Like my father, Fred also had been imprisoned in a concentration camp—in his case, it was Buchenwald.

Our accommodations could not compare with those that the Schwarz family found. They lived near the top of a beautiful apartment building on the entrance overlooking the harbor in Havana. They spent money as if there were an endless stream of cash that would flow into their pockets. But they had applied for a quota number before we did, and their number was called after only three or four months.

It was fortunate for the rest of us that they emigrated quickly, because my parents fretted constantly about money and didn't need the stress of watching the Schwarz family spend. My parents didn't know if the $6,000 that Uncle Otto had deposited in the National City Bank of Havana was going to last or not. They also hadn't fully understood that our needs would increase because we could not take much clothing or other amenities with us. The only way to know if our funds would be sufficient was when our quota numbers were called. Either we still had money or we didn't.

Jews by law weren't even allowed to work in Cuba under its revolutionary government. The only way you were permitted to work was if you opened up a store or business and hired Cuban workers. The law was very strictly enforced. Only a few Jewish refugees attempted to open businesses, although there were a decent number of businesses owned by Cuban Jews. There was also a collection of Cuban Jews who tried to organize a kibbutz and engage in communal living. They cleared jungle at the southern tip of Cuba and formed their kibbutz. However, such living was of no interest to European refugees. It eventually failed.

Of course, although I heard my parents' complaints about money, I was too young to realize what it all meant. I got fed. I got clothed. I had running water and a toilet. What did I have to worry about?

ငလ

Our house was in El Vedado, the bustling center of the Cuban capital. It was a destination of wonder for a 12-year-old. You could smell the salt from the ocean from our house as we were only two blocks from the shoreline.

I would spend time on El Malecón, an oceanfront walkway that was first constructed at the turn of the twentieth century when the United States ruled Cuba and then gave the country its independence. Americans today have just about forgotten what Cuba was like before Fidel Castro, although perhaps memories have begun to come back since the restoration of diplomatic relations in 2015. The island was developing as a playground for the American well-to-do with luxury hotels, nightclubs, and casinos. Our house was two blocks from the López Serrano at the corner of Calle 13 and L, the most modern building in Havana and its first skyscraper. The white art deco building was the tallest in the city, standing about ten stories high, plus a few more if you count the tower, although it was so gigantic to me that I could have sworn it was at least twice as tall. In later months, a friend of mine convinced me how fun it would be to sneak in and have a little mischief. We would ride the elevator up and down and back up all over again for as long as we could stand it or until we got caught. That was our idea of a thrill.

Several blocks away, on the Malecón itself, stood the majestic Hotel Nacional de Cuba overlooking the harbor where we had disembarked from the *Iberia*. If you remember a scene from *The Godfather II* where a bunch of mob bosses met at a Cuban hotel, it was based on an actual meeting that took place there in 1946 (fortunately, several years after our departure).

The beaches of Havana were beautiful. There was actually one section called the "American beach" where we were able to go swimming. In fact, it was the only place we were permitted to go swimming by the government. We would take a bus on occasion and go in the water.

Of course, you couldn't swim on the beach and play in a skyscraper all day, and we couldn't afford the entertainment available to American tourists. So we made our own entertainment and filled the day as best we could.

I remember my father buying those fragrant Cuban cigars he had talked about, cutting them into two or three sections and puffing on them through the day as he sat out on the porch. Also, the longer we stayed, the more European Jews we found in the same limbo as we were, awaiting their quota numbers to enter America. The tendency is to bond with people who are from similar backgrounds, and we did. They would come to visit, exchange stories, play Skat, and eat Aunt Herta's tasty cooking. It was through listening to these conversations that my sheltered existence began to dissipate. The adults would talk about Kristallnacht and relatives left behind. They would talk about news heard on the radio and news learned from letters received from Europe about conditions there for Jews. Inevitably, one family would discover it knew friends or relatives back in Germany of another family.

Even though we had cramped quarters, we did get a little income by taking on a tenant with the last name of Baustein. He was a newly divorced American who had immigrated to Cuba to make a living as an English teacher. But he also spoke German, so he could communicate with us. He enjoyed living with us because the arrangement meant his time was filled in the company of others instead of coping with loneliness. After a while, we began to ask Mr. Baustein to teach English to us and the rest of our extended household. He was glad to oblige. We passed many hours on the porch outside doing just that. I learned English not only from Mr. Baustein, but also at a school I attended where English was spoken. I had a very hard time at the school even with Mr. Baustein's help. Still, by the time I got to the United States, although I wouldn't say I was good at English, at least I was able to make myself understood.

My parents, on the other hand, only picked up a smattering of English words and phrases. Adults generally have a harder time picking up a new language than children do. I say "generally," though, because Uncle Hugo was the exception. The first thing he did when we got to Cuba was buy himself a dictionary. He started with the A words and went all the way through the Z words. He studied every word, and he knew the meaning of every word. The only thing he didn't know was how to put them together in a sentence.

Later in life, after he and his wife had built up a large baby clothing business in New Orleans, he would have high-level meetings with corporate executives and other bigwigs and unfurl sentences that only an author like James Joyce or William Faulkner might be able to dissect. As for anyone else, these sentences could only be deciphered if you brought along a dictionary. Fortunately, because he was a friendly, handsome gentleman—who had a lot of lucrative business to offer—the meetings generally went well anyway.

CR

If only so many of our Jewish brethren had found their deliverance as we had—and God forbid what our fate would have been if we had left Germany only three months later. The Hamburg America Line, known as Hapag, continued to send ships bearing refugees to Havana, including a return visit by the *Iberia* in early May. On Saturday, May 27, its sister ship, the *St. Louis,* arrived. But only a minimal number of passengers were allowed off due to what was rumored as strong pressure from the US government. There were 937 passengers, including friends of my mother, stranded on board. Among them was Elisabeth (Lisel) Hass, who at age 25 was on board with her then-husband Leo and who would later marry into my family. My mother knew Lisel's parents, whose last name was Katz, from a clothing business they had operated in Rhaden. They sent salesmen in cars and buggies all over the farmland to sell their goods.

The impasse continued and the passengers still were not allowed to disembark, not even to be held in detention at Tiscornia. Cuban officials had revoked their landing permits. The ship sat in the harbor for days, close enough to freedom that we could faintly make out their silhouettes from the shoreline.

On one of those days anchored in the harbor, we communicated with Lisel and her husband and exchanged greetings by shouting across the water. With so much pressure being exerted by Jewish organizations, our expectation was that we would be welcoming Lisel and her husband into our home in a day or so.

The voyage of the *St. Louis* was to become the subject of the movie *Voyage of the Damned*. The following Friday, the ship left the harbor. At one point, it came within sight of the lights of Miami. It then circled back, sailing around the entire island of Cuba as passengers prayed for a resolution. Nevertheless, governments around the world refused to take in a shipload of Jews, including the US government and President Franklin Roosevelt.

On June 6, the ship was forced to return to Europe after a deal was reached where Great Britain, France, Holland, and Belgium agreed to each take a portion of the refugees. But for many, this meant their eventual doom and being sent to concentration camps. All of those countries except Britain were overrun by the Nazis a year later. According to the US Holocaust Memorial Museum, 254 passengers met their deaths at the hands of the Nazis.

Roosevelt was beloved among America's Jews during his lifetime, but those of us with connections to the *St. Louis* placed the blame for its fate squarely on him. We believed the United States used its influence to persuade Cuba not to permit the refugees to land for fear they would make their way to American shores just 90 miles away. In fact, according to the Holocaust Museum, the passengers were caught in a squabble between different corrupt factions in Cuba. Also in play was a tide of antisemitism that was rising due to the arrival by this point of about 2,500 Jews. I was shocked to discover that reports about the impending voyage of the *St. Louis* triggered a large antisemitic demonstration of 40,000 people in Havana on May 8, five days before the *St. Louis* sailed from Hamburg. We never felt anything but welcome during my time in Havana and knew nothing of this outburst.

As for Lisel and her husband, they survived the war in hiding in Holland. After the war, they were able to immigrate to the United States. Her husband later died, and my cousin Fred Jellin married her in the 1960s.

☙

It was around the time of my thirteenth birthday, in late 1939, that I made my first Jewish friend, Edgar Cohn, or Eddy for short. It was Eddy who accompanied me on my adventures up and down the elevator of the López Serrano.

My fellow German Jewish refugee and I showed how being a naïve kid can work to your advantage. I thought I was rich because I owned a roller skate. Not a pair of roller skates, mind you—just one skate. Eddy also owned his own roller skate. We could have taken turns with the skates and watched one another. But we wanted to skate together. So each of us put on his one skate and went up and down the streets that way. We became known as Havana's one-legged skaters. Come to think of it, we were pretty damn good at it.

We also made and shared some homemade kites with long, trailing tails. We would take them to the Malecón along the harbor and fly them until the arrival of other kids with kites. The favorite sport of the local kids was to tie razorblades to the tail of their kite and try to slice the other kids' kite strings. We were better one-legged skaters than defenders against razorblade-wielding kite flyers. We fell victim to this kind of warfare so often that we finally capitulated and gave up.

അ

As late August 1939 arrived, my parents' and friends' discussions turned from stories about the good old days to the horrors of the new day. My father and other refugees listened to American radio broadcasts with dread as Germany was threatening Poland, while Britain and France made it clear they would send no troops to help if there was an invasion. Britain was trying to stir up antigovernment sentiment by dropping leaflets over German cities. But having lived under Hitler for so long, my father had a clear picture of what lay ahead.

"There is no doubt in my mind that Germany will overrun Poland in no time at all and that a victorious people are in no mood for revolt," he wrote in his diary on September 1, 1939, unaware that German tanks had rolled across the Polish frontier early that morning. "It is very sad to think now of the fate that awaits those poor Jews living in Poland."

By the middle of September, the fighting was essentially over and Poland had been partitioned into two by Germany and the Soviet Union, which had invaded from the east. With disgust my father would hear the names of Hitler, Göring, Himmler, Hess, and others on the radio and react violently, still wishing that Germany would remember its former greatness from when he was a soldier. He said that in his younger days, these men would be arrested as criminals.

On the night of September 22 began Yom Kippur, the holiest day on the Jewish calendar. It is a holiday where many different meanings are entwined. It is the Jewish Day of Atonement, when we pray for forgiveness, yet it is also known in the liturgy as *Yom Hadin* (Day of Judgment). We gathered at one of our neighbor's houses that served as our makeshift synagogue and found ourselves praying this holiday with fervor we had never felt before. We wanted God to render judgment against the Nazis who had forced us from home, but we wanted God to look after aunts, uncles, and cousins we had left behind in Germany as well.

Yet Yom Kippur, too, is a day of *yahrzeit*, or remembering the dead. During our service, my father urged us to pray even for the gravesites of his parents back in the tree-lined, serene Harrl mountain ridge of Bückeburg. He feared that if their resting places were disturbed, perhaps my children and grandchildren and future generations would forget them and their heritage. Still, it was the decreasing flow of letters from our German kin that worried us more than anything. We feared for their survival as well as their ability to provide for themselves even if they could survive. *Avinu malkeinu kasveinu b'sefer parnassa v'chalkollah* (Our

Father, our King, inscribe us for your protective care and the ability to sustain ourselves) we sang in one of the most important Hebrew prayers of the Jewish high holidays.

∝

After the Jewish holidays passed, a milestone was arriving in my life. I was about to turn 13, meaning it was time for my bar mitzvah. It wasn't like it is now with parties in a huge catering hall, DJ's, balloon arches, and ice sculptures. But this was still a big deal, marking my transition to manhood.

My father found a substitute cantor by the name of Lewisohn who had emigrated from Hannover, Germany, with his father, where they had been schoolteachers. He tutored me for several weeks on how to chant my Torah portion, as well as the additional reading from what is known as the haftarah.

I knew that my bar mitzvah was going to be on Saturday, November 11. But it took until November 10 to find out where the bar mitzvah would actually be held because we had a royal snafu right just before the big day. Our contingent of German Jewish refugees got together regularly on Friday nights to welcome the Sabbath as well as on Saturday morning. But our "place of worship" was always somebody's house. Fortunately, or so it seemed, we were able to arrange to hold the service in what was named the American Temple, a reform congregation for wealthy US vacationers. I practiced there for the big event. But my father lost it when he came to see me practicing and found out that they didn't wear a tallit (prayer shawl) or a yarmulke on their heads.

Fortunately, my bar mitzvah was to meet a better fate than cramming everyone into a house. The director of an English business school heard of our predicament and, at the last moment, was able to make a large classroom available for us to hold the service. Like the butcher who would take no payment for matzo, he, too, would take no payment for our use of the room.

The service was not what we had expected back when we were in Germany, where family and friends would have come from Lüdenscheid and throughout the countryside to be there. It was both solemn and festive.

Yet even though any other day I would have been curled up in bed because of a terrible head cold, I sniffled my way through the service in a way that my father said would have made my grandparents proud. The Torah portion was *Lech Lecha*, in which it says the following: "And the Lord said unto Abraham: 'Get thee out of thy country and from thy kindred and from thy father's house.'" I can still see my father, with tears in his eyes, explaining to me the significance of this event and the parallel of the story to the present time.

Many of the congregants came to our house afterward, where they were offered wine, liquors, cognac, homemade cookies, and cake. The *sude* (festive meal) was later in the evening. We had invited a few friends, numbering 20 in all. Many made speeches. With the serving of fruit salad, pies, and cakes, this joyous and genial gathering lasted until well after midnight. For a remembrance of this day, the congregation presented me with a beautiful siddur (prayer book), which I have in my possession to this day.

The days passed with our English lessons from Mr. Baustein, our occasional excursions to the American beach, and our Sabbath services to occupy us. Then, in the middle of 1940, we received a letter. Our quota number had come up. We were going to America.

CHAPTER 4

A New Life in New York

Americans have certain expectations about immigrant stories. One is that immigrants will feel overwhelmed with emotion upon entering New York Harbor and seeing the Statue of Liberty for the first time. Another is that they will describe how Lady Liberty symbolized their entrance into a land of freedom and opportunity.

But my first memories of New York? The one that sticks out in my mind involves vegetable shortening. One evening shortly after our arrival, after we had settled in the Morningside Heights neighborhood on the Upper West Side, I accompanied my parents on a walk to Riverside Drive. Suddenly, I felt a sensation of shock and awe as I saw a huge sign across the Hudson River in New Jersey for a product called "Spry." The letters on that sign were larger than any I had ever seen, and they illuminated the night. The sign blinked with the words "Spry for Frying" in a bright white light and "Spry for Baking" in a red light that reflected in the Hudson's waters. That Spry sign, to me, was about the most impressive thing I'd ever seen.

My appreciation for the liberty and opportunity that America has provided me and my family aside, I feel I have to question the books and articles that talk about Europeans arriving in America and welling up with tears at seeing the statue. Jews from Germany, Poland, and Russia did not know about the statue. The symbolic value is something Americans have attached to it; we weren't aware of it at all. While I can picture some eastern European immigrants saying, "Hey, that's a terrific looking statue," as they drifted into port, they wouldn't have had thought to connect it with liberty or freedom. So I hope it doesn't disappoint you that while I remember the first time I saw the Spry sign, I really can't recall if I even noticed the Statue of Liberty upon arriving from Cuba.

With that said, one thing you couldn't fail to be impressed by as we viewed the city from the harbor waters was the size of New York. Cologne was a large city when I lived there to attend school, much larger than Lüdenscheid, which had perhaps 40,000 to 45,000 people. But those towns were mere pebbles compared to New York and its tens of thousands of buildings. That's not to mention the height of the buildings themselves. Not long after we settled into New York, we were walking in the financial district when, upon reaching Wall Street, my mother stopped as if a hammer had suddenly appeared and nailed her feet to the sidewalk. She was petrified. The reason soon became readily apparent. She was afraid one of the skyscrapers would fall on her.

"How can it stand up like this?" she said with her voice trembling. "Whoever saw anything like this?"

There was no convincing her it was safe to walk there. We had to take an unscheduled detour.

I have to admit, although I never worried about a building falling on top of my head, it took me a long time to get over my own sense of awe. When I was around 30 years old, in the mid-1950s, I had to go to Wall Street to survey buildings for my air conditioning business. Many times I found myself stopping to gaze upward and saying to myself, "How is it possible that this building could ever be made? How did they get the bricks up that high?" Looking back, I admit I should have been more impressed by the buildings than the Spry sign.

After the ship docked in Brooklyn, my family and Aunt Herta and Uncle Hugo's clambered down the walkway and were met by representatives of the American Jewish Joint Distribution Committee (JDC) and the Hebrew Immigrant Aid Society (HIAS), the main organizations for supporting immigrant Jews. Decisions that would affect the course of our entire lives suddenly had to be made in a moment's notice. They came to us and offered a choice. We were welcome to settle in New York, but émigrés received support for only two years if they did so because the competition for jobs and housing was so fierce. But they were providing an incentive to those willing to migrate elsewhere in the United States. Families accepting the offer would receive help for as long as they needed until they were self-sufficient.

Aunt Herta and Uncle Hugo took a few minutes and decided it was worth a chance. They took up an offer to have HIAS settle them in New Orleans. None of us had any idea where New Orleans was except that it was in the United States and was nowhere near New York; the lucky among us might have remembered from history class that Andrew Jackson won a key battle there in the War of 1812. But they flourished in New Orleans in a way that no one could have foreseen.

Uncle Hugo spent years in the southern heat as a peddler, going door to door selling maid's uniforms. But the simple act of kindness of having his wife make a small garment whenever a baby was born into a customer's house proved their foundation for the American dream. The garments were so lovely that customers asked if his wife would make more, for which they would happily pay. Soon a small business started. Over 10 to 12 years, it grew into two factories employing several hundred people. The company was called Cuté Togs, and it developed into one of the leading baby and children's wear businesses in the country.

But my own family wasn't about to venture out of New York when it was where most of the refugees dwelled. At any rate, we did have some family members who, even if they were too young to help us, could at least offer the comfort of knowing somebody in this bewildering new place.

One was my cousin Edith, a relative on my mother's side. She had immigrated to the United States earlier in hopes of starting a new life. In those days, it wasn't just the JDC or HIAS that met you at the dock. There were also people who greeted ships in hopes of hiring servants or other kinds of help. Edith was met by a Jewish family looking for an au pair to take care of their daughters. She worked for them for a couple years until she made a little money and learned enough English to get by.

Another cousin who had arrived in the late 20s or early 30s was named Ruth. Aunt Klara, my mother's sister, and husband Leopold Jelin (spelled Jellin for those making it to America) had six children. But with money scarce during the Depression, she and her husband found they could not afford to feed six children. So when the eldest, Ruth, turned 18, she was put on a boat and sent to America to make her way on her own. Ruth worked as an au pair and house help. But she would wind up marrying well. Her husband was a man named Dr. Fred Daniels, who performed military research on radar and how radio waves functioned in space. A highlight of his career was collaborating with Dr. James Van Allen, one of NASA's great pioneering astrophysicists, in discovering what became known as the Van Allen radiation belts surrounding the Earth. In one of those odd coincidences sprinkled throughout my life, Van Allen worked directly on the launching of America's first satellite (shortly after the Russians launched Sputnik) with the US space program's leading figure, Wernher von Braun, a former Nazi scientist whom I had been assigned to accompany during my time in the army.

Sadly, Aunt Klara, Uncle Leopold, and their youngest child would not live to see how Ruth and her husband's life developed. Records list her parents as dying in the Theresienstadt concentration camp. But one of their sons, Curt, became a soldier in the American Army, and toward the end of the war discovered their actual fate upon returning to his hometown of Herne in western Germany. In an oral history from 1977, he said his parents were supposed to be sent to a concentration camp but instead were placed on a cattle train that was sealed and gassed. A sister, Else, tried to escape to England, failed, and was killed at about age 25 ahead of the Russian advance in a camp near Riga, Latvia, toward the end of the war. He said her death was because she was in charge of the gold knocked from dead people's teeth and that she knew where the gold was.

There was one other cousin on my mother's side, Henry Oppenheim, son of Uncle Hugo and Aunt Herta, who arrived in New York before us, leaving on a Kindertransport, or children's transport. Shortly after Kristallnacht, the British decided to waive immigration requirements and accept 10,000 Jewish children as refugees from the Nazi regime, with many destined never to see their parents again. But although these were the largest, they were not the only Kindertransports; there were others as well, going to different countries. This smaller one was organized right after Kristallnacht by New York Mayor Fiorello LaGuardia, who was known for his Italian heritage but actually was born to a Jewish mother. He called on all city administrators and private citizens to take in Jewish children who had escaped on these transports and made their way to New York. Henry was adopted by a man named Maurice Davidson, commissioner of water, gas, and electricity in the LaGuardia administration. Henry lived with him and was sent to an excellent high school. When in 1940, his parents Hugo and Herta emigrated to the United States and moved to New Orleans, Henry did not want to join them. But they insisted, and to Louisiana he went, where he lived until he passed away in April 2013.

଒ଽ

Upon hearing our decision to live in New York, one of the JDC representatives took us right from the ship and drove us around to get us a bit acclimated. Then he took us to the Automat. Talk about things you would never see in Germany. The Automat was the 1940s version of fast food and dazzled our eyes and palates. Freshly prepared food sat behind individual windows, and you could pick whatever you wanted by placing money in a coin-operated machine and lifting the window. After buying our meal, the JDC representative arranged a room for us to stay in, which we would sublet from another family. He drove us there and left us on our own.

Those first months in New York were both exciting and frightening. At least I could understand a bit of English. But my parents could not speak the language, which was quite a barrier when you are trying to learn your way around a colossal city. They often found themselves standing on a street corner feeling utterly disoriented, not knowing which way to turn, because the brownstones and office buildings all started to look the same. I don't think my parents ever ventured more than ten blocks in any direction from that first apartment. It was much, much longer before they dared to set foot on the subway and explore other parts of Manhattan.

Initially, of course, we could not distinguish one neighborhood from another. But the JDC had directed us to an area populated by other immigrants like ourselves. The most common destination for new immigrants had been Washington Heights, nicknamed the Fourth Reich for its concentration of German Jews and located in one of Manhattan's northernmost sections. But when we arrived, many were being directed to the nearby Upper West Side, including the Morningside Heights neighborhood that also had a large population of German Jews and includes the Columbia University campus. Many thousands of German Jewish immigrants called these areas home.

We couldn't stay long in the one tiny room that we were subletting, so after a short while, we began hunting for new accommodations. With various Jewish organizations helping out by providing addresses for other apartments, we were able to locate one where the rent was reasonable and, as long as we took in boarders, would work within our JDC-supplemented budget.

We wound up at 529 West 111th Street, apartment 64, on the top floor of a six-story brownstone. It would be our home until 1961. It had six rooms: three bedrooms (including a tiny one called a maid's room), a dining room, a living room, and a kitchen. Unfortunately, because of our need to sublet space, we still would have to fit into just one room for our sleeping quarters. But even though we would have to share the additional living space, it was better than not having it at all.

My parents and I wound up converting the living room into our bedroom. We rented out the dining room and the three bedrooms to various boarders. It was only when we began to work and earn our own money that we didn't need boarders anymore. It would take about three years until my parents got their own bedroom and I got mine, although we did keep one boarder for about ten years. He was an old man named Werner, a German Jewish refugee. He had no family because they all had died in the Holocaust. We didn't mind having him as he was an amiable fellow, and he only lived in the maid's room anyway. He was grateful to live with us and have people he could talk to in his native language. All of the boarders were older, single men. It wasn't difficult to find renters. The Germans had created a supply of refugees who had lost their wives and children and somehow surfaced in Manhattan, and the JDC and other organizations were guiding and supporting them with housing just as they had assisted us.

Despite the tight quarters, everyone got along reasonably well. The boarders became part of the family. We had a schedule for the bathroom. If someone had to go to work early, he used the bathroom first. If someone needed the bathroom urgently, the schedule was changed by knocking repeatedly on the door and pleading, "Let me in, let me in!"

Often the boarders would share meals with us. We offered them breakfast for 10 or 15 cents, and dinner for 30 or 35 cents. My father and I shuddered if my mother ventured into the kitchen. I believe boiled water was her finest culinary feat. But our boarders either had lost their taste buds on the ship to America or were the most polite people ever born, because they praised everything placed before them on the table as long it was ample enough to quiet their rumbling stomachs.

Fortunately, my father was fairly skilled with a stove and an oven and cooked a majority of the meals. We ate on a strict budget, which meant eating rice in forms that required creativity. He conjured up one concoction that consisted of rice, raisins, and milk. A deluxe version also included rhubarb, cinnamon, and sugar. Another meal option was rice and cheese. These rice dishes constituted the entire meal, other than perhaps some soup. Believe it or not, they tasted delicious.

We ate a good amount of the less expensive meats, particularly hamburger and lamb. One of our staples was sausages, known as wurst, which were kosher style (although none of us actually kept kosher) and was sold in a horseshoe shape. There were beef sausages shaped into a heavy knockwurst, and *weisswurst,* or white sausages, which consisted of veal. You could boil your sausages in a big pot with peppers and onions and have them as an *Eintopfgericht,* or one-pot meal. To this day, I still eat sausages prepared this way. Just the spicy aroma brings me back to our old apartment and the warmth of my parents.

Of course, it was important to cut costs any way possible. In the words of my father, if you put one nickel on top of another nickel on top of another nickel, before you know it, you have saved a dollar. One way to save was to limit the amount of toilet paper used. My parents used to cut newspaper into squares that were the same size as the toilet paper. Then they punched holes through the squares, threaded them with string and hung them by the toilet seat. Voilà, you now had "two-ply" toilet paper. Of course, we quickly learned the proper grip so the ink from the newspaper only got on our hands and not our sensitive behinds. I have to admit there probably weren't that many refugees who went to such extremes. But at least there was always reading material while you were on the toilet—in very short snippets.

The cash provided by the JDC kept us afloat in those early days. In addition, it provided us small slips of paper, which you would call coupons today, which certain grocery stores accepted in exchange for receiving cash later from the JDC. Storeowners with any foresight accepted the coupons, because their businesses blossomed from the resulting expansion of their customer base. As time passed and refugees started to have their own money, they tended to keep shopping at these stores out of a sense of loyalty to those who accepted them during their time of need.

The Upper West Side was a melting pot in the truest American sense. In addition to German Jews, there were also large populations of Italian and Irish, as well as nonimmigrant Americans. The groups did not fight among one another. Although we were a minority, we never felt as if there was any antisemitism in the community. The streets teemed with people speaking German as if they were still planted thousands of miles away in the hills of Lüdenscheid or the busy streets of Cologne. The difference was the addition of Italian and English in the mix.

When we did venture into Washington Heights, however, we would rarely hear any English. The whole place seemed populated only with German and Austrian Jews, so the German language was all we ever heard. Visitors really could lose themselves for a moment and think it was Europe. We certainly did not hear Yiddish, either. That was the language of eastern Europeans. That's the language we would hear if we took the train over to the Jewish neighborhoods in Brooklyn or the Bronx.

Our neighborhood consisted largely of six-story apartment houses with elevators, including the building where we lived. There were also a couple of banks, a few stores with stockings and ladies' wear, a beauty parlor, a barbershop, and a good number of butcher shops. There was just one small bar with a restaurant attached it, but we never went there because eating out was a luxury we couldn't afford.

Thinking back, I am not sure how America stacked up to my initial expectations. In the haste of our departure from Germany and then busying ourselves getting accustomed to Cuba, I don't think I really formed expectations. Honestly, I didn't live that much differently in America than in Europe except for the change in language. I walked the street, went to school, and, other than that, I mostly stayed home.

Actually, I did have one expectation where I found America disappointed me. As a young boy, I was dying to see my first Indian with a feathered headdress. I thought Indians were going to be running up and down the street. I remember once asking somebody on the street where they were. He didn't even know what I was talking about.

CR

Back in the 1940s in Manhattan, it was not unusual to have a knock on the door every day or two from someone wanting to sell their wares. These days, the typical reaction is to say thank you and close the door as quickly as you can, or tell everyone to be quiet and hide until they go away. But back then, we looked forward to that knock.

In fact, the Fuller Brush man was an example of why we welcomed what would now be considered an intrusion. He was the salesman we anticipated the most, arguably one of the most important men in the Upper West Side. It wasn't the items he sold for personal and house care, although we bought some on occasion. It was that he kept us informed of all the goings-on in our community. He always offered warm conversation and, from his travels on foot, he could relay all the major events of the day, ranging from politics to new people moving into the neighborhood to the birth of a baby.

He wasn't alone in being a source of company and conversation. An elderly man from Vineland, New Jersey, came each week to sell us raw eggs from a large straw basket. We always wondered how none of them ever broke. Another entrepreneur came with loaves of challah every Friday afternoon, baked that day in his wife's kitchen, which we would use that night for our rituals to welcome the Sabbath. A butcher by the name of Pollak would make his weekly round with the knockwurst and weisswurst I enjoyed so much, eventually building a lucrative sausage business. And one man came regularly to sell homemade chocolate.

We could have bought these products from any number of stores in New York. But that wasn't the point. We were a *kille,* a community. The Depression was just coming to a close and life was hard for us all. But in our world, we never gave any thought but to take care of our own in any way possible. We were poor when it came to money, but rich in brethren.

CS

My father's first job was making deliveries for a millinery shop. He usually got lost on the subway on his last delivery and tended to finally make it home around 10 p.m. He would, of course, receive a hero's welcome for his efforts.

I, too, needed to contribute financially, even though I was only 14 when we arrived from Cuba. That meant we could not afford to be picky. My father found a job for me that I could go to after school. An old acquaintance of my father's had bought a five-story townhouse on the Upper West Side that served as an apartment building. He was looking for someone to go on errands and help around the house. I reported for work five days a week after school. My responsibilities were simple enough: clean and mop the floors, sweep the steps and stoop outside, clean up after coal deliveries (which often left me looking like the chimney sweep played by Dick Van Dyke in *Mary Poppins*), and take care of the needs and welfare of the tenants with any other simple errands they might require.

Still, the work felt rewarding, as the single ladies who occupied all the apartments in this five-story building took a shine to this refugee kid. When I returned after buying their groceries and cigarettes or picking up their dry cleaning, there was always a reward of a nickel or dime, which was a substantial sum in the 1940s. Every day before I went home, one or another of the nice ladies would give me some fruit or cookies to take home. My parents were very thankful for all the kindnesses bestowed on me, and I, of course, was full of praise for these lovely ladies.

About six months into the job, my father had some free time and said he wanted to come for a visit and see how I was doing. If any of the tenants happened to be home, he would take the opportunity to personally thank them for their warm, generous attention. On the day my father visited, I proudly introduced him to one and all. Many welcomed him into their apartments and invited him to socialize. I felt the visit couldn't have gone better.

So you can only imagine my surprise that evening after I came home when my father informed me that this had been my last day on the job. I was stunned and angry, and to make it worse, he didn't offer any explanation. My mother was in total agreement, adding only that no offspring of hers would ever work in that kind of establishment. It took my father three years before he finally explained why he ended my employment. The ladies were hard-working, self-employed women, but in a profession that was not strictly kosher. Thus ended my involvement with these ladies of the night.

☙

Just as we sought out a synagogue in Cuba to help us acclimate to a new land, my parents again found it critical to find a congregation where we would be comfortable. In June 1941, just as we were settling into our new neighborhood in the Upper West Side, a group of refugees arrived from Luxembourg after their rabbi, Dr. Robert Serebrenik, had miraculously negotiated with Adolf Eichmann, the architect of Germany's "Final Solution" to exterminate the Jews, for permission to emigrate. They founded Congregation Ramath Orah on West 110th Street, just around the corner from our apartment. Within a year, out of gratitude to the rabbi for saving their lives, they purchased a former Unitarian church built in 1921—a brick neo-Georgian building with four stone pillars carved into the façade—to call home.

There were no Jewish community centers or counterparts to the YMCA at that time. All we had were our synagogues. That is where we went not just to pray but to congregate and be with people like us. They were a place for even the simplest social outings like playing cards, including Skat. My family made Ramath Orah a home and so did our boarders. Like us, they found refugees who had lost loved ones and could share their common fears, hopes, and frustrations. The congregation consisted entirely of German and Luxembourg Jews.

We did go to synagogue on the Sabbath and kept all the holidays. But even so, I wouldn't consider religion itself to have been a focal point of my life. Like many kids, religion was less important than being with friends. In fact, the second there was a snowfall on the Sabbath, I was faced with the choice of going to services with my father or going skiing with friends. Well, my father went to shul and I went skiing. My father didn't like it, but there wasn't much he could do.

☙

As the center of our community, Ramath Orah was also the means of my finding another place of employment. As with any congregation, there is generally someone whom the rabbi can call upon when he needs an infusion of cash or any money-related favor.

At Ramath Orah, that man was Willy Schwab. In Germany, I don't think my parents would have had much to do with him. He was a cattle and horse trader, a poorly regarded occupation. However, it did turn him into a wealthy man, and he left Germany early enough in the 1930s that he was not stripped of his wealth as we were and was permitted to bring his money with him.

I'm sure that my father must have figured that after my unwitting entanglement with the ladies of the night in my first job, what better way of finding me employment could there be than asking Rabbi Serebrenik for guidance? Right away, the rabbi concluded that Mr. Schwab was the man on whom to call. Schwab at this time owned a small plant on the corner of 58th and Broadway for manufacturing foam rubber items. Among his products were small pillows and powder puffs used for makeup.

The plant had cutting machines and presses on the second and third floors. My job was to come after school and operate the freight elevator, sending foam rubber up from the basement whenever it was needed to the floors where manufacturing was done on cutting machines and presses.

Well, I began the job just as winter began. This was a severe winter and one day was particularly blustery. I couldn't shake the chill . . . until I got into the nice, warm basement of the plant. It was so cozy that I laid down on a stack of foam rubber and fell fast asleep. When they needed the foam rubber, cries went out of "Where is Fred? Where is Fred?" Nobody could find me until, at last, they checked the basement and found me lying comfortably on my pile of foam rubber. As I understand it, it took them quite a while to rouse me from my snooze.

I knew the consequences wouldn't be good, considering how my father and the rabbi had collaborated to get me this position. Well, I was hauled in front of Willy Schwab. He spoke no English, but he spoke German loud and clear.

"I'm ashamed of you," he scolded. "And how ashamed your father must be that he has a *Schlafmütze* (sleepyhead) as a son. You can't work for me anymore. You're fired!"

I was sent home to face the wrath of my father and then the rabbi. I'm not sure which was worse. They eventually got over it, but from that day on, I was greeted by Rabbi Serebrenik as the *Schlafmütze*.

But there would always be work, especially with other family members to bail me out. A cousin on my father's side, Herman Arends, along with his brother-in-law Harry DeJong and their wives, had started a small business making change purses, cigarette cases, and wallets. They personalized them by gluing on names or initials. These items took off like wildfire and it was difficult to keep up with demand. I worked for them in every capacity that a young, eager kid could. That lasted until Herman and Harry were drafted into the army.

But I did land one job where I managed not to fall asleep or accidentally be in the company of women of disrepute. That was with Klinger Dental Laboratory on 42nd Street, delivering false teeth to dentists all over town. The owner, a Jewish gentleman from Brooklyn, kept me on for three years.

ᘓᣝ

Although I learned a good bit of English while still in Cuba, it wasn't nearly enough for me to feel prepared when I enrolled in public school in New York. I attended P.S. 165, just four blocks from where we lived. I had extraordinary difficulty. There were no special classes back then to help immigrants. The government did not cater to us. We simply had to do the best we could. Such schooling would be unimaginable today, but that's how it was done at the time.

Kids back then were no different than they are now. Instead of playing with me, the American kids would make fun of me because of my German accent and the way I tripped over English words and phrases. They had their own groups of friends and cliques. They rarely made an effort to welcome me and generally did not feel comfortable with me. But then, the feeling went both ways.

I flunked twice in public school and was held back because I could not understand directions well enough (being held back is a rare treat that's much more unusual today than during my teenage years).

There was no television back then to help us absorb the new language. Radio wasn't helpful, either. First of all, what immigrant family right off the boat could afford a radio? Heck, I couldn't even buy ice cream when the vendors came by because we couldn't spare the three cents. Furthermore, even if you could listen to someone else's radio, you couldn't see anything to place the words into any context. I can't imagine how much easier it is today. Parents today can pick up a computer for a few hundred dollars and buy software to help sort out language troubles if they choose.

But the JDC did provide immigrant families one program to help us learn English. Every two weeks, we were sent one nickel per family member. That paid for us to attend the theater, where Hollywood would be our best teacher. We "studied" English by watching Humphrey Bogart and John Wayne (although preferably not picking up their mannerisms, I suppose). The Flash Gordon serials, starring Buster Crabbe in his battles against evil Emperor Ming on the planet Mongo, proved enjoyable English tutorials, as did Mickey Mouse and Woody Woodpecker cartoons. I found it to be so impressive. You could watch a serial that continued with a new episode every week, then comics, then the newsreels, and then the coming attractions. And there were always double features. So when you went to the movies, you could easily hunker down there for anywhere from three to six hours. Ironically, I had more real English instruction in Cuba than in the United States.

But what English I did master as an immigrant I knew better than Americans who grew up here. Don't think for a minute that I am bluffing, either. My current lady friend, Nikki, was born and raised in Philadelphia and is always asking me how to spell words for a crossword puzzle. I'll give you another example from around 1960. Because my store was only a few miles from Columbia University, I thought it would be a good idea to hire some students who were looking for summer work. But whenever I asked them to write a letter, I had to rewrite it. They could not write a halfway decent letter or even use proper spelling. And these were Ivy Leaguers! I may not write the best letter, but there won't be any mistakes in it.

The funny thing, though, is that to this day I often do not think in English. I very often find myself fumbling for a word and only able to think of it in German. Doing mathematics is a whole special obstacle course. I cannot add numbers in English. I have to say the numbers to myself in German. That's even with learning a good amount of more advanced math in America. I'm willing to guess that this malady is quite universal. Later in life, when my wife helped me in my air conditioning business and we had a customer and had to add up the bill, it was like a comedy. The customer added in English, my wife (who grew up in Panama) added in Spanish, and I added in German. After a conference and several minutes, we would finally arrive at the same answer.

After graduating P.S. 165, I registered at Chelsea Vocational High School and sought training in a machine shop in hopes of getting into the tool and die field. After three months, I had second thoughts. I wanted to get to college, and this wasn't the way to get there.

So I transferred to George Washington High School in Washington Heights. Among the immigrant refugees was a fellow named Henry Kissinger, who went on to become President Nixon's national security adviser and secretary of state. He was a bit older than me, so I can't offer you much insight into Kissinger's early years other than to mention he was something of a grump and not terribly communicative.

As I headed into my teenage years, our money started to grow just a little bit. That meant we could splurge on a radio and listen to many of the music programs. I loved much of the classical music, although I confess to also giving a lot of attention to The Lone Ranger, and The Shadow as well. I still find the words from the introduction to the show ringing in my head now and then: "Who knows what evil lurks in the hearts of men? The Shadow knows!"

We also still received our JDC nickels for the movies. Once in a while we could use those nickels to go to a concert instead. Sometimes I would visit a museum, but if it had an entrance fee, forget it! That was definitely a luxury we couldn't afford.

The *Aufbau,* a German-language newspaper for the Jewish community, was the Facebook or Twitter of its day and became a means of fostering the formation of social groups. We would arrange with friends in Washington Heights to have an afternoon of coffee and cake. Wherever the *Aufbau* was read, people would read it and organize musical afternoons or evenings, and they would perform for themselves. There were many German Jewish organizations with sufficient talent to mount a singing group.

There were dancers, too. I don't know if this also happened in Europe, but in New York, for sure, all young German Jews, both girls and boys, had to take dancing lessons. The lessons were all taken at the same German dance studios. Well, calling them studios would be flattery, because they were simply dingy rooms like any other except for the playing of music. But I distinctly remember

Mrs. Peretz's studio and how she taught all the graces of politeness, not only on the dance floor but in life.

In fact, some European customs carried over for many years longer than you would expect. When you said hello to a lady, you bowed and said hello. I even had some older friends who, in the German fashion, would click their heels and bow when saying hello. They carried this habit with them even into their 50s and beyond.

High school was a struggle for me as well, but fortunately enough, my brain started to operate on a faster gear. I made up the ground from being held back and was able to graduate from high school on time. But it wasn't a college or career that awaited.

CHAPTER 5

A King on Riverside Drive

When we arrived in America as immigrants, we had few options if we wanted to enjoy the outdoors. We couldn't afford to head for the Long Island beaches or the amusements of Coney Island, let alone venture off for a vacation in the Catskills. We didn't even consider it wise to go spending the little money we had on subway rides to other parts of New York City. We thought it was a good idea to have money for food.

But we did have Riverside Drive, which snakes alongside the Hudson River, separated from the water by a narrow stretch of wooded paths called Riverside Park. And on Riverside Drive, there were perhaps 40 to 50 blocks of benches, including the Behrend bench, presided over by my father Herman, dispenser of wisdom, lifter of spirits, and fervent practitioner of the art of conversation.

Technically, the benches that stretched for many miles along Riverside Drive belonged to the city of New York. But that was solely in the legal sense. Although Central Park was only a few blocks away, to our fellow poor immigrants and us, Riverside Park offered all the amenities you could ever want. It was beautiful, shaded by large trees and a wide walkway between the northbound and southbound roads. The breezes off the Hudson would cool us on those humid, broiling New York summer days on the weekends and make us forget we were in the largest city in the United States. If we wanted to head over to the riverside, we could see that beloved Spry sign as well.

These waterside amenities meant the benches on Riverside Drive were prime real estate. Immigrant families in our area between 96th and 115th Streets staked out their benches aggressively. These were *their* benches. Each family had a bench, and members of the family would sit on that bench and that one alone. There were no markings, but everyone knew where everybody sat. Of course, if we visited people at their bench, they would gladly shift over to clear a space for us to sit. But nobody would dare think of sitting on someone else's bench if he or she saw it empty. What if the family came down and found someone occupying their spot? That would be an unthinkable affront.

It may seem like a strange mentality to take "ownership" of something that doesn't belong to you. However, it wasn't at all to us. New immigrants owned nothing. They had no fancy cars or lavish apartments. But if they could lay claim to this little oasis of beauty, then that made them feel like they did own something precious.

We were no different. We had our Behrend bench. And because of my father, the Behrend bench was one of the most popular spots on Riverside Drive. His optimism was magnetic. Not only did he look at the bright side, but he was quite literally incapable of pessimism. He just wasn't built that way. People came up to him when they needed cheering up and would rarely leave disappointed. He was a natural, an excellent raconteur. He could quote Goethe, Faust, and all the well-known writers and poets of the day from Germany. He would be at the bench through the day, holding court, reminding people how good they had it in America and to be grateful for the opportunities it presented.

I can remember one German Jew in his 40s rambling on about how poor his family was since coming over to America. He complained how his apartment was small, how he had to share it with a boarder who complained about everything from the food to the shower, how he could barely scrape together money for the other bills besides the rent with the small amount of money that the JDC provided.

"How am I supposed to live like this day after day after . . . ?" the man said before my father interrupted the stream of self-pity.

"What are you talking about?" my father interjected. "You have your children. They're living with you. You know how many were killed in the concentration camps? Be thankful!"

The man settled down. I don't know if he realized my father was right or that he would be crazy to argue with a man who commanded such respect. But he calmed down and the conversation shifted to other topics.

Another downtrodden gentleman came by, puffing on his cigar as he made small smoke rings that wafted in the air. His shirt was stained in spots from ashes that had crash-landed there in the past. He, too, was muttering about his worries—living in a single room as a boarder, forced to make due on sausages instead of good meats. Again, as was his style, my father stopped the man before he could go further.

"How lucky you are!" he said. "You're smoking a cigar. How can you afford that cigar? It had to cost you at least five cents. Do you realize how lucky you are?"

He was the strength behind my mother. He had to be. Life was so different in Lüdenscheid on the Zeppelin estate. We had our servants and cooks and a driver. We had our silk and bedding store, where there were even more employees. He and my mother could afford to go away to the spa at Bad Eilsen, where they refreshed themselves in the warm springs and took strolls in their finest clothes along the tree-lined promenades. My parents were the driving force behind our small congregation in Lüdenscheid, with my father serving as the synagogue's final president before the Germans scattered our brethren.

Then, all the wealth was gone, taken by the Nazis. Also gone was the stature that my parents enjoyed. There was not a neighbor to be found who resented them for their wealth because they were so active in the community and giving of their time.

Yet with everything that we lost, my father's cheerfulness never deserted him. It is this cheerfulness that made it easier for my mother to face the loss of comfort and accept what life had given her in Cuba and then in the United States.

His ability to maintain this disposition was not a surprise. He carried that attitude through the First World War, when he saw combat on distant battlefields. He refused to get down and bemoan his wounds. He always mended and returned to fight again. Millions died on the battlefields of that war. He was always one bullet or land mine away from death over the entire four years of that war. Yet he also had the camaraderie and the lasting friendships that develop during endless hours in the trenches. He had the sense of purpose and duty that came from fighting for the fatherland. He looked at danger, sorted through the facts in his own unique way, and decided things could still be worse. This sense of optimism and gratitude for the good in his life carried him through every circumstance.

The only time I ever extracted any acknowledgment that anything other than positivity shone in his life came during one conversation that drifted to the concentration camps and the memories of the beatings, endless hours of manual labor, and threats of the guards.

"Papa, how did you have enough strength to survive in the concentration camps?" I asked. "Look at what they did to you. So many people died there. How did you ever make it through?"

In this circumstance, it seems, optimism and pessimism played no role. There were just facts . . . and faith. He knew he could die there. He had no way to know that my mother and other members of my family were working hour after hour to exhaustion, assembling funds and pleading with Nazi officials to arrange his release. This time, it was just a matter of hanging on.

"Fritz, I know my time in the concentration camp compared to others was very short," he said. "But still, it took every bit of my strength to pull through. It was God's will and my belief in God. If it hadn't have been for my strong belief in God, I never could have done it."

❧

My father never approached the same level in his professional life that he had held when running our store back in Lüdenscheid. He was always taking whatever odd jobs came his way, including that first job with the millinery shop that left him wandering aimlessly around New York in search of his delivery destinations. The only sustained work he found in New York was as an office boy, or office man, if you want to be kind about it. He worked for Heilbrun Import and Export at 60 W. 42nd Street on the 12th floor for many years. He and Mr. Heilbrun had been friends in Germany, and when my father struggled to find work, his old friend took care of him.

Now, my father's skills as a store manager never came back into use in this position. But he always labored hard through the day. His job consisted of wrapping packages and taking them to the post office. Sometimes these were exceedingly large bundles that had to be wrapped and walked over despite great exertion, whether on humid 90-degree days in the summer or on freezing days in the winter with icy sidewalks. He also was a jack-of-all-trades, doing anything and everything needed in the office. It was the barest of existence. He earned perhaps ten dollars a week. But my father was practically jovial. He might as well have been king of Prussia. We could afford to have our Passover Seder with matzo for the whole family. He could afford to put together a small gift basket for Hanukkah. Life was good. My mother and I welcomed my father with warm embraces whenever he came home from work, because we were proud of him and loved him. That was all he needed.

On such meager wages, there was little in the way of entertainment that my parents could afford. But on 42nd Street, between 6th and 7th, there was the very Automat where the JDC representative had mesmerized us within hours of disembarking from our ship to New York. We were enchanted by it on that first day in America, and we kept it near our hearts—and stomachs—forever.

However, my father could not afford to buy any food there. Every day he would go with a sandwich and an apple that my mother packed, and he would sit in the Automat and get a glass of water. There were big buckets full of lemons, so he would take a couple slices and squeeze the juice into the glass. To that, he would add two spoonfuls of sugar, sit at the table, and sip his homespun lemonade. He'd also grab a napkin, and perhaps a straw if he felt daring.

This went on for about five months, sitting with a homemade sandwich and a store-concocted lemonade, perhaps chatting with other customers if they were so inclined, until a manager came over.

"I recognize you," the manager said. "You come here often. It's nice here, and you like to eat lunch here. But I never see you put a dime or nickel in the slot."

My father was very embarrassed and struggled to respond. He was afraid his Automat days were about to end, and he was ashamed that he might lose face in front of this man of authority. He looked for the right words to say, but it was difficult under pressure to find them when instinctively only his native language came to the surface.

"You don't know English well?" the manager asked.

"No, English bad," my father responded straightforwardly.

"Well, where do you come from?"

"Germany."

"You're one of those refugees that came over?"

"Yes, yes. I was."

"Well, how did you come here?"

My father then managed to explain in his choppy English that he had been in a concentration camp.

The manager smiled. "Don't you worry," he said. "You can come here any day you want to sit at the table and nothing will go wrong. If you want to have a coffee, I'll buy you a coffee."

My father brightened. The Automat would remain with the Behrend bench as a place of home-like comfort. The manager would come chat with him as best he could from time to time. Until my father retired, he went to that Automat every day. No one ever bothered him, even on days the manager wasn't there. Clearly, the manager had kept his word and left instructions to leave this immigrant alone.

ℭℛ

No man could spend time in a concentration camp and come away unchanged. Those days inside the barbed wire led to life lessons that he taught me as I grew from a teenager into a young man. While he always encouraged me to look forward with a sunny point of view, a strategy that I've carried with me in nine decades on this earth, he also told me to keep one fact in mind: antisemitism will always be present, and it might be a threat to your way of living, even if not necessarily to life itself.

He was more worried about the possibility that America might turn against its Jews in the way that Hitler did initially, through legal means. Hitler only did in the 1930s what European countries throughout history had done before: banning Jews from going to schools, boycotting Jewish goods, preventing them from entering certain occupations, and so on. There was a shared feeling among refugees, etched in their souls through hundreds of years of oppression, that Jews would always face an uncertain existence. What happened in a highly intellectual, civil country like Germany only reinforced that point. To us, Germany was a much more cultured place than the United States, and if it could happen in the fatherland, it could happen in our new homeland, too.

America looked after its Jews in some ways, but hostility toward them still ran as a dangerous undercurrent, keeping fear and suspicion in the back of our minds. New York, with its hundreds of thousands of Jews, was an enclave where it was natural to feel the antisemitic bite much less. But it was always there. Many colleges were known to be verboten to Jews: my friends talked about going to the City College of New York, but no one even thought to apply to Harvard, no matter how brilliant he or she was. Aunt Herta and Uncle Hugo, who immigrated to New Orleans, felt it much more deeply there as Jews were something of a rarity.

Immigrants, in fact, learned to develop a social life among themselves in response to the chilly welcome from others. Given the language barriers they faced, coming together in this manner was the only natural outcome. But I have to admit that were class differences even within the tribe. Immigrants from western Europe formed different bonds than those from eastern Europe.

People who immigrated here from Germany, Austria, and Czechoslovakia, just to name a few countries, tended to have more formal schooling and worked largely as merchants and professionals, while immigrants from Russia, Poland, Bulgaria, and other countries in the east tended to be peasants who lived in poverty and struggled to get by in the old country. In addition, those from eastern Europe spoke Yiddish, while those from western Europe did not.

Our particular group tended to have been businessmen in Europe like my father, although there were lawyers and doctors in the mix, too. They would gather to form associations and clubs. These were not casual groups that you joined and forgot about, only to remember a few times of a year if you got a reminder in the mail. These groups gave life a social fabric. People like my parents attended these clubs on a regular basis and would visit one another's homes and form friendships. These new friendships not only made life easier, but also pleasant, as immigrants did not feel like strangers in this strange land. They felt right at home.

But while eastern and western European Jews didn't mix much, other social divisions we once knew in Germany were cast aside under the common stresses we now faced. Carpenters and plumbers might suddenly find themselves being friendly with a person who owned a large business such as a store, factory, or warehouse.

In the mid-1940s, for example, when I was off in the army, my parents met a couple at a Quaker resort in New York. This particular Quaker group spurned social convention and invited refugees to go to their farms in the countryside because they felt sorry for them and wanted to do something nice. These were all German Jews, and while at the resort, my parents struck up a friendship with a couple by the names of Iwan and Elizabeth Cope. Back in Germany, the Copes—who financially exceeded us by extraordinary amounts—would never have accepted my parents as acquaintances, let alone as friends. But it goes to show what happens when you are thrown together under different circumstances. They were the closest of friends for the rest of their lives. Iwan and my father played Skat for years and years, to the point that each had a deck buried with him in case they needed it in the hereafter.

My father's advice to beware of antisemitism affected how my future played out. He told me not to be an academic, which is the path I would have followed in Germany.

"Learn a trade that might be useful wherever you might go," my father said to me, "whether that's a shoemaker or a carpenter, or an electrician or a plumber. Because if you know a trade, you will always be able to make a living and support a family."

That's exactly what happened. This was back in the day when even a high school dropout could earn enough to pay the bills for his family. Going to college was not something you had to do to survive, as it is now for the most part. That's not to say I wouldn't have attended college if I could, but there was a two-year wait after my army discharge. It wasn't a realistic option to wait. So instead, I eventually learned to repair televisions, and then air conditioners. His advice served me well as I was able to support my wife and two children and retire comfortably when I sold my business in 1991.

I never thought that my father was telling me to be a lesser man when he told me to learn a trade. It was just a different path. And I never thought any less of him for not attaining the same professional stature in America that he had when he managed our store in Lüdenscheid. I admired him because he took any job that was handed to him, and he worked at it with pride. I know this outlook is so much different than we see today. I certainly don't expect my grandchildren to grow up and say they want to go to a technical school to learn how to fix cars. However, it should not be that your reputation depends so largely on college. Learning a trade and taking care of your family—there is nothing more honorable than that.

ℭ

There was one place where my father received the same level of honor and respect as in our native land. That was Congregation Ramath Orah. As I got older, I kept company with a number of the Luxembourgers who had escaped Eichmann's wrath, some of whom wound up as my skiing companions.

These refugees had been in the jewelry business, dealing in diamonds and gold, and eventually returned to their original lines of work. They fared better financially than my family.

But these Luxembourgers were a welcoming group. They didn't look at my father as someone who ran errands for a living, as someone who struggled just to find a few dollars for his family to get by. They saw my father as he saw himself, a well-spoken man accustomed to a role of leadership, a former president of a congregation, a man who could converse on anything from the opera to Talmud. People sought him out for advice and friendship. He joined them as a founding member.

More than just being a friend, he was always the type of person who would take charge if something needed to be done. He established himself as one of the central figures of Ramath Orah, being elected to a spot as a board member and taking charge of the *chevra kadisha*, which is a duty that no one aspires to but is one of the most sacred in the Jewish religion. It is considered one of the great mitzvoth, or good deeds, to attend a funeral or otherwise honor the dead, because one performs the act without the possibility of receiving anything in return. My father never thought twice about making sure this duty was taken care of—going with friends to the home of the deceased to ensure that, as required in the Jewish tradition, the body would not be left alone. They would play cards throughout the night, and then in the morning they would wash the body to prepare it for the funeral director.

My father often gave lectures before the congregation. He even received the honor of giving the *D'var Torah* (a brief commentary about the week's Torah portion) on the Sabbath, a duty generally performed by the rabbi. The rabbi grew very fond of my father and our entire family. I recall during the Sabbath, at times when my mother was ill, how Rabbi Serebrenik would come to our apartment building just to pay a visit and keep her company. To this day, Ramath Orah has my father's shofar (a ram's horn blown during high holiday services) and a wimple, which is a fancy cloth used to wrap the Torah, that my parents received when I was born.

When my father died in 1958, the impact that he had on his community could be seen in the number of people who turned out to pay their respects at the funeral hall on West 79th Street. Mourners came out by the hundreds. It became so crowded that finally the doors to the adjoining room had to be opened up just to accommodate them all.

CR

The tears shed on the ship ride from Europe to Cuba tell much about how my mother differed from my father, and how critical my father was to her well-being. While my father's optimism was as steady as the stars in the night sky, her outlook on life dimmed once everything she knew was taken away from her. A woman who had never been a pessimist became one with the loss of her standing in the community. She was no longer the woman that people would call upon to lead charitable fund-raisers or to collect winter coats for the poor or food for the hungry. Now, we could only survive by accepting the charity of our fellow Jews.

My father's encouragement was the main thing that kept her spirits up in Cuba and through our early years in America. She followed my father's lead as they formed social bonds with German and Austrian immigrants in the Upper West Side. Although they joined music groups, book clubs, and intellectual discussion groups, she was never the same.

This difficulty in adjusting to a new lifestyle persisted for many years, through all the time she lived in Manhattan. My father never got to see her be like her old self again. However, she did finally get there in the last seven or eight years of her life when she entered a German Jewish retirement home in Queens, which was occupied by former refugees like herself. Finally, at last, she felt very much at ease because she was completely among her own and the staff there treated her warmly. That's when she started to live again in relative happiness until she passed away peacefully in 1971.

Although she missed the comforts of the Zeppelin property and the cooks and drivers, she was a most unpretentious woman. She could get by without those luxuries in Manhattan, much as she missed them. In Lüdenscheid, my father had been fond of buying her jewelry from time to time. As he walked along the streets near our business, he would wander in a jewelry store, and if he saw a ring or a broach that he thought she would like, he bought it. She thanked him profusely with hugs and kisses. But she would never wear it. She kept the jewelry in the original boxes. Lüdenscheid was a city of working-class people. She didn't want them to see she was so much better off than they and could afford gold and diamonds.

We paid a heavy price on the culinary side when we left Europe due to my mother's problems with cooking. If she made chicken, it resembled any meat other than chicken. If she made toast, she burned it. She was the only person I know who could burn water. You think I'm kidding? I distinctly remember one time when she put a kettle on the stove. When she came back for the hot water, the kettle had melted and begun to turn black. The water had evaporated.

But she was never meant to be a domestic. She had a sharp mind and was a businesswoman of unmatched brilliance. She had kept the books for our silk and bedding store, and when I went out into the business world, she oversaw my finances as well. I always had to laugh when a row of numbers had to be added up. She would run her finger up and down the column three times and she would arrive at the sum. She could calculate as fast as the adding machines where you had to type the numbers in . . . even faster. She would be finished before you were done entering them. She was the one who encouraged me to put most of my earnings in a bank.

"If you put it in your pocket, you'll spend it," she would tell me. "Just put your money in the bank. You don't know when you might need it."

She was an extremely warm woman. If there is one thing that both my parents impressed upon me is that there is nothing more important in life than family. You love them, respect them, do whatever you can for them. Of course, I do the same for my children. That's how I honor my parents, because none of us would be here if they had not sacrificed everything for us to escape to this country.

But I certainly wasn't the spoiled brat of Germany anymore. Once we were here in America, my parents sat me down in a hurry and explained that things were different now. Once I was old enough, if there was anything I wanted or needed beyond the basics, I would have to start providing it for myself. And in their later years, they fully expected me to be their sole support. That was the European way, and fortunately, there were many New Yorkers in need of repaired TVs and air conditioners.

Image Gallery

A Passover Seder in the home of Fred Behrend's grandparents in Bückeburg, Germany, in 1903. From left, his aunt Grete (Margarete), grandmother Mathilde, grandfather Gothelf, father Herman.

Herman and Grete (Margarete) Behrend in the traditional costume of Bückeburg, circa 1915 (*above*).

Wedding program of Else (Fred's mother) and her first husband, Robert Stern, on May 18, 1914, just two months before the start of World War I. Robert would be the first casualty among residents of the city of Lüdenscheid (*left*).

Synagogue in Bückeburg that Gotthelf Behrend's family attended.

The main house at the Zeppelin compound in Lüdenscheid, home of the Behrends until they fled Germany in 1939.

Fred as a baby with grandparents Mathilde and Gotthelf Behrend in 1927.

Fred Behrend's parents Else and Herman walking the grounds of the Bad Pyrmont spa in Germany in the 1930s.

Stadt Lüdenscheid

den 3. April 1933

Sprechstunde der Redaktion 11—12 Uhr vormittags
(Nachdruck aller Lokal- und Kreisnachrichten verboten.)

Ruhiger Verlauf des Boykott-Tages

Der von der NSDAP anberaumte Boykott-Tag am Samstag ist in der ganzen Stadt ruhig verlaufen, d. h. außer den angeordneten Maßnahmen sind keine anderen zu verzeichnen. Natürlich war während des ganzen Tages eine gewisse Spannung zu beobachten, aber Sensationslüsterne kamen nicht auf ihre Rechnung. Die größeren jüdischen Geschäfte hatten bereits um 10 Uhr geschlossen, vor die anderen wurden die Posten gestellt, die Schilder mit den vorgeschriebenen Aufschriften trugen.

Die Firma Robert Stern hatte in eines ihrer Schaufenster ein Plakat gestellt mit der Aufschrift: „Der erste amtlich gemeldete Kriegsgefallene Lüdenscheids war der Jude Robert Stern, Gründer dieser Firma". Daneben fand sich der „Lüdenscheider General-Anzeiger" vom 13. September 1914, in dem die Stadtverwaltung damals diese Mitteilung machte. Die Polizeiverwaltung hatte gegen die Aufstellung des Schildes nichts einzuwenden, aber die Entfernung wurde von den SA-Posten dennoch gefordert. Der Geschäftsinhaber schloß daraufhin das Geschäft. Der Vorgang zog eine riesige Menschenmenge an.

Bei der Geschäftsstelle der „Volksstimme" entstand ein Auflauf, weil dort Flugblätter verteilt und versandt worden sein sollten. Es handelte sich dabei aber nur die Ausräumung des Geschäftslokals, das von der „Volksstimme" aufgegeben wird. Eine Haussuchung fand am Nachmittag gegen 4½ Uhr aus demselben Grunde im Gewerkschaftshause statt. Der Umstand, daß die Zugänge dabei von der SS und SA besetzt wurden, lockte auch hier eine große Zuschauermenge an. Nach Durchführung der Haussuchung wurden mehrere Personen, darunter der Gewerkschaftssekretär W. Bürger, der Stadtverordneter ist, in Schutzhaft genommen. Ebenso wurden drei weitere SPD-Stadtverordnete in Schutzhaft genommen und zwar G. Jüngermann, Hch. Knepper, Aug. vom Orde und der Angestellte der „Volksstimme" W. Statkwinkel. Die Ansammlung am Gewerkschaftshause hatte zeitweilig einen bedrohlichen Charakter angenommen.

Members of Fred's family enjoying the grounds of the Zeppelin compound. Back (*from left*): his aunt Grete Behrend, father Herman, mother Else, and Fred. Seated: grandmother Ida and uncle Otto Oppenheim. Otto was primarily responsible for the Behrends' escape but did not survive (*above*).

Article in the *Stadt Lüdenscheid* on April 3, 1933, discussing the Day of Boycott affecting Jewish stores and what happened at the Robert Stern store. Herman and Else Behrend caused a stir in their efforts to combat the boycott, placing a sign in the window that Robert Stern was the first soldier to die in the Great War from the city of Lüdenscheid and that the establishment's owner was his widow (*left*).

The Bückeburg gravestone of Gotthelf and Mathilde Behrend, Fred's grandparents.

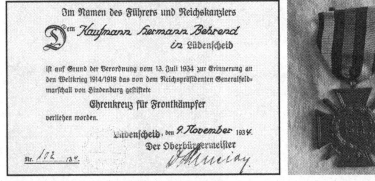

The certificate (*left*) presented to Herman Behrend that accompanied the Cross of Honor (*right*) awarded to front-line soldiers from World War I. Dated November 9, 1934, the certificate ironically begins, "In the name of the Führer and Chancellor of the Reich." President Hindenburg prevailed over Hitler in allowing non-Aryans to receive it.

Other medals awarded to Herman Behrend included, from left to right: the Iron Cross, the Cross for Loyal Service (from the prince of Schaumburg-Lippe), the Cross of Honor for military service, and a Wound Badge.

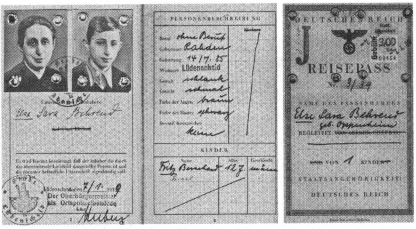

Passport for Else Behrend, mother of Fritz Bernhard "Fred" Behrend. This also served as Fred's passport. The cover is stamped with a large "J" for Jude, or Jew. The document shows how the middle name of "Sara," assigned by the Nazis to Jewish females, was given to Else, and how "Israel," assigned to Jewish males, was given to Fred.

Detail from Else and Fred's passport: "Fritz Bernhard Israel."

Immigration identification document for entry into Cuba, showing the Behrends arrived on the *Iberia*.

Herman Behrend in uniform for the German Army during the First World War.

A winsome Fred Behrend at age 12 in Cuba around the time of his bar mitzvah.

Fred Behrend in uniform for the US Army at the end of, or shortly after, World War II.

Fred, 12, with father Herman and mother Else aboard the Iberia en route from Germany to Cuba in 1939.

Fred (*top center*), mother Else (*directly to his left*) and father Herman (*far left*) with other family members in front of their house in Havana.

Fred Behrend teaching German prisoners about US government. Behrend was an instructor in the army's "Intellectual Diversion" program at Fort Eustis, Virginia, in 1946. As seen on their uniforms, prisoners at the time were known as PWs instead of POWs.

Fred Behrend and a captured German V-2 rocket at White Sands Proving Grounds, New Mexico, in 1946.

A captured V-2 German rocket at the launch pad at White Sands, New Mexico.

Wernher von Braun (*left*), who directed Germany's V-2 rocket program and is considered the father of the American space program. The German inscription on the back of the photo (*right*) reads, "Herr Behrend, for a remembrance of the beautiful and productive days in Ft. Bliss and White Sands. Prof. Dr. Wernher v. Braun."

Fred's mother Else and father Herman (*left*) with friends Elizabeth and Iwan Cope on a trip to visit Fred's family in New Orleans in the 1950s. The Copes' industrial plant was seized by the Nazis. Iwan fought for two years and won it back postwar in the German courts.

Fred Behrend (*far right, back*) and wife Lisa (*second from right*) with others gathered in Lüdenscheid in 1990. They had come for the dedication of a plaque honoring the city's Jews, who had fled during WWII. Mayor Jürgen Dietrich is pictured at bottom right.

Fred Behrend, pictured in 1991, showing the site, outside the former Zeppelin compound in Lüdenscheid, of his failed childhood escapade of riding down the steps on a bicycle. He was found bleeding and unconscious.

The family's Robert Stern store, which sold silk and ladies' fabrics in the 1930s, and during a 1991 visit to Lüdenscheid. It had become a pet store.

Fred Behrend, in 1991, outside the twelfth-century castle in Bückeburg that was home to kings and princes of the state of Schaumburg-Lippe. He had played in its palatial grounds as a child.

Fred Behrend (*seated*), daughter Evelyn (*standing, left*) and Bückeburg Stadt-direktor Ernst Möller (*second from right*) in 1991, as Fred reads a passage from the diary of his grandfather, Gotthelf.

Philipp-Ernst, prince of Schaumburg-Lippe (*center*), greets Fred Behrend's daughter Evelyn and son Andrew in a 1991 visit to the Bückeburg castle.

Fred Behrend (*left*), with Lüdenscheid Mayor Jürgen Dietrich, in 1991 holding a seventeenth-century megillah, a family heirloom, being donated to the city museum.

Fred Behrend and Ruth Westheimer share a light moment during a party in recent years.

Seder plate used by the Behrend family since 1710. The only known interruption in its usage over the centuries came in the years immediately after the family fled Germany. Photo by Tyler Hanover.

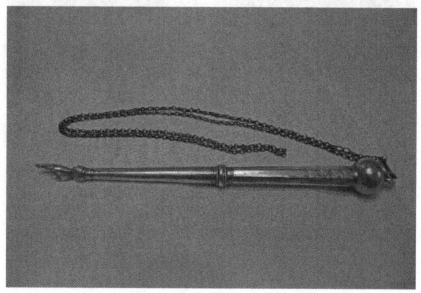

The yad (pointer used for reading the Torah) found by Fred's father outside the city's destroyed synagogue during Kristallnacht in 1938. It was most recently used by Fred's granddaughter, Marisa, during her bat mitzvah in 2014. Photo by Tyler Hanover.

CHAPTER 6

Tales of the Unlikely Soldier

I never gave it a thought when I received the order to report to the base hospital in Fort Bliss, Texas, for a physical on December 1, 1946. It seemed like typical army nonsense. I'd received a physical when I was drafted and would get another on the way out, too, but if the army wanted to waste some doctor's time by having him check my pulse and make sure my leg kicked upward when tapped by a reflex hammer, that was fine with me.

But after spending a lot of time reading eye charts, sticking out my tongue, and answering questions to fill out form after form, I was directed into a room where an officer stood waiting for me. He stuck out his arm and thrust an envelope containing my discharge papers and $300 cash in exit pay into my hand.

I *was* out and I didn't even know it.

"You are now honorably discharged from the US Army, effective immediately," he said, leaving me thunderstruck. "I have been ordered to instruct that you must leave Fort Bliss in 24 hours. If found on base after 24 hours, you risk arrest and possible imprisonment."

Word sped around camp faster than the captured German V-2 rockets we were test firing into the desert sky. *Everybody* seemed to know that I was out, and I can't even imagine what kind of treachery they thought I had committed. When I asked a buddy of mine who was a pilot if I could fly out with him to start heading home, even he looked at me as if I'd contracted rabies.

"Are you kidding? Get away from me!" he said.

I have to admit that when I first entered the army in July 1945, any sensible person could have predicted that the army and I would not part ways on the best of terms. I was lazy, an incurable mischief maker, and never met an officer to whom I wouldn't talk back.

But despite all that, fate somehow catapulted this schlub of an enlisted man into having more responsibility and adventures than some generals I had encountered. I had run a POW camp, instructed hundreds of German soldiers on how to trade fascism for democracy, translated the highest levels of Nazi war correspondence, been attached to the German scientist who would become the prime architect of America's space program, and been present for the rocket launch that resulted in history's first pictures from outer space—all before my twentieth birthday. I didn't expect a parade, but all things considered, I figured my discharge would be more ceremonious than this.

∽

My mother didn't say anything, but the sadness in her soulful eyes communicated everything. Even my father, the German army veteran, couldn't hide his trepidation as we opened the letter from the local draft board in January 1945.

Throughout the refugee community, mothers and fathers knew it would be the children who paid the greatest price for living in this new land by going off to serve in the American military. But when we escaped from Germany with our lives, the furthest thing from my parents' minds had been the possibility of placing their only child in harm's way. Now, just six years after fleeing our beloved homeland, they had to worry that I might have to face the bullets of Hitler's army.

My own feelings were mixed. I had no desire to go into the army. But if I had wound up entering the military at this point, I suspect the army would have found a boy with an attitude more to their liking than the troublemaker they got. I actually had a bit of a gung ho attitude. I may have been a sheltered little boy inside the walls of Graf Zeppelin's former estate back in Lüdenscheid, but now I fully understood the Nazis and the terror unfolding outside those walls. If I had to serve, I wanted to go to Europe and do some damage in the country where my relatives and friends had been murdered or imprisoned in concentration camps.

Still, although I had just turned 18 a couple months earlier, I had not finished high school. Regardless of our feelings about the war, my parents and I agreed that a boy should at least have the right to finish high school before risking his life. We needed to concentrate on persuading Uncle Sam to at least allow me to get my diploma.

We placed the job in the hands of my father, who went off to appear before the local draft board to argue on my behalf. To our relief, the board agreed with us. He came home with a draft deferment.

Of course, if there's one thing where American greatness is unsurpassed, it's red tape. Uncle Sam sent me another draft notice that April. This time, my high school principal came through, writing personally to the chairman of the draft board. The board ruled, again, that I could complete high school.

I think my good "uncle" was standing at the mailbox, waiting to pounce and send out draft letter number 3 as soon I completed my final exams. On June

19, 1945, when my personal greetings from the president of the United States arrived, I had to accept. But at this point, the war in Europe had been over for more than a month. We were still fighting the Japanese, but what quarrel did a Jewish kid from Germany have with them? My gung ho attitude had fizzled like a bottle of Coca-Cola left open for a week.

The state of my morale didn't bother the army big shots enough to keep them from taking me, of course. In fact, just as they had been in too big a hurry to draft me, they were in even more of a hurry to get me into uniform. I didn't even have time to attend my own graduation ceremonies as I readied to report. My official induction took place on July 17. I was placed right onto a bus to Fort Dix, New Jersey, for six weeks of indoctrination.

And how memorable that initial indoctrination into the army was. When I arrived, I was placed in the hands of a roughly sixty-year-old master sergeant who took it upon himself to make sure we had a proper initiation. No sooner had we traded in our civilian clothes for fatigues and been assigned bunks than he invited us behind the barracks to introduce us to the game of craps. Then he introduced us to something else—the feeling of being suckered. Within 45 minutes, he relieved us of all our money.

From Fort Dix, we went on a two-day train ride to Camp Claiborne, Louisiana. When the good Lord created hell, he must have had this place in mind. It had every kind of flying and crawling insect. It also had every form of snake, plus a generous helping of rats and bats. Our barracks were built on stilts about 10 to 12 feet off the ground to prevent water—and unwanted creatures—from getting inside when it rained. And did it ever rain.

If I still harbored any illusions about whether the army and I were going to get along, they disappeared right away. It's not that I was terribly unhappy. From the moment I set foot in Cuba in 1939, trading in my walled, friendless Zeppelin-estate past for more than a year of Latin-style freedom and new friends, my outlook had brightened. It was as if I had been in a dreary dark room all my life and now emerged into the sunshine. My innate optimism and happy nature were set free.

But with that taste of freedom came a lack of enthusiasm for the life of a soldier. After my induction, my father wrote me letters saying how proud he was to have a son as a soldier and giving me instruction on how to behave in the army, such as showing respect to my sergeant and my superior officers. But his admonitions didn't register one bit. If you gave me an order, I'd talk back. I was in trouble regularly. I can't begin to tell you how many times I landed on KP duty, peeling potatoes and washing dishes. I started to think I owned the kitchen.

It didn't help that I had no qualifications whatsoever for the role for which I'd been selected. In its first display of wisdom, the army decided I belonged with the combat engineers' demolition squad. Part of the job entailed blowing up anything that could be mined or rigged to explode. That included booby-trapped weapons left on dead soldiers, including sidearms, daggers, and especially ceremonial swords. The experiences of World War II were much like those faced by our troops in Iraq and Afghanistan.

Fortunately, soon after I arrived at Claiborne, the United States and Japan signed a peace treaty. The war was over. I wouldn't face live fire or blow up explosives under combat conditions. Though my training would go forward, I had dodged World War II.

My avoiding the war was best for all involved, because I never belonged anywhere near hazardous material. The instructions for setting explosive charges in my initial training were explicit: walk away after planting the charge. Never, ever run because you might stumble and be wounded if you're too close to the explosion. After attaching a long fuse and lighting the charge, I was proud to report to my instructor about my "successful" mission. He, however, wanted to know whether I'd heard the charge go off. I had to admit that I'd bolted so far and fast that there was no way in hell I would have been able to hear a thing. He told me to get my ass back there and check. The charge had exploded, but that didn't save me from two days on KP duty.

Hand grenade instruction went even worse. An intimidating 30-year army man had the job of showing me how to throw one. "Pull the pin and lob it over the wall. Understood?" the sergeant snarled. I did exactly as I was told. I pulled the pin and lobbed it over the protective wall. The *pin*, that is, not the grenade. He looked at me in disbelief, ripped the grenade out of my hand, and threw it over the wall just before it exploded. Back to KP . . . again.

Crazy as it was, I didn't mind going to KP, because I ate the best food. Army food for the enlisted men was not exactly like mother's cooking, you know, and being in the kitchen allowed access to the food set aside for the camp commander. You would be amazed how often a juicy steak managed to work its way onto my plate.

I was given a two-week respite from my training snafus when I was sent to Camp Polk in Kentucky. Stationed here were the remnants of a unit called the "Ritchie Boys." During the war, friends and relatives, including my cousin Curt Jellin, had trained at Fort Ritchie, Maryland, as volunteers for a special role in fighting the Nazis. These Jewish refugees of Nazi terror were given lessons on intelligence and counterintelligence. They worked behind the front lines in Europe from the invasion of Normandy through the German surrender in May 1945, interrogating prisoners and gaining critical information for the war effort. In an oral history, my cousin described being trained in psychological warfare in broadcasting, then serving in late 1944 as a broadcaster to Germans between midnight and 6 a.m. to sow doubt in their leadership and try to break morale.

Obviously, with the war over, I would not get to be a Ritchie Boy, but I did receive my own version of spy training. I was given instruction on how to determine if German POWs were telling the truth or not when speaking with them. We also learned to interpret their letters, trying to read between the lines to see if there were hidden meanings. But it was only for two weeks, and after that, it was back to Camp Claiborne to complete basic training. I'm glad it was peacetime, because I can't imagine having come up with a single piece of useful intelligence after that rapid-fire course.

Mercifully, for the safety of others and me, basic training was drawing to a close. It appeared any further KP duty would be conducted across the Pacific. With duffel bags in hand, we boarded our convoy of a dozen trucks to head out of camp and start our trek to occupied Japan.

A group of soldiers, however, sped in a jeep to the camp gate and intercepted us before departure, stopping every truck. Soon, they stopped mine. The rear flap opened.

A soldier called out, "Is Private Behrend on the truck?"

"Yes," I replied in bewilderment.

"We have to talk to you," he said. "You are wanted back at headquarters."

All kinds of thoughts raced through my head. My heart pounded out of my chest. What kind of trouble was I in this time? After all, this couldn't be my ordinary KP trouble if they were pulling me off a truck that was taking me on the first leg of my journey halfway across the world. I went to retrieve my duffel bag, which had all my worldly possessions, but the soldier told me to leave it, as I would be able to reclaim it later. We hopped in their jeep and drove to camp headquarters.

When I arrived, however, I discovered I wasn't in trouble after all. After sitting outside the camp commander's office for a few minutes, a captain ushered me inside. The officers began to ask questions about my background and knowledge of German, wondering if I could speak, understand, and write it fluently. I told them yes. I told them that I was born in Germany and my parents knew virtually no English, so German was the only language spoken in my house. I also said that I frequently read German-language newspapers and books. Then they asked me to sit outside, where I waited for a half hour.

When I was summoned back in, they told me that the commandant of the POW camp at Camp Claiborne had suddenly been stricken with appendicitis and died. They needed someone new to run the camp for a short time who could communicate with the POWs until a proper German-speaking replacement officer could be found.

That someone was an 18-year-old private named Fritz "Fred" Behrend.

I later heard through the grapevine that they had identified me for the job through the most scientific analysis. That analysis consisted of poring through personnel files at headquarters looking for someone with a German name, going in alphabetical order. Thanks to me, they were able to stop at B. It's a good story, but in reality, I have a feeling my training in psychological warfare from my course at Camp Polk had something to do with it.

As for my duffel bag, and the worldly possessions contained therein, I never saw it again. I can only guess that it is enjoying an endless vacation in the Far East.

CR

I was flabbergasted. I was barely out of high school. What I did I know about being in charge of anything? I had as much knowledge about running a POW camp as a cow about playing piano. Yet there I was for the next month, in charge of hundreds of prisoners. My father wrote to me with advice on how to treat these Germans. Again, I ignored his advice, but for once with good reason. Had I listened, I would have gotten an instant court martial.

I discovered there were a number of prisoners who were not Nazis or willing soldiers of the Third Reich. Many were young kids, just like me, who never had the desire to die for the Führer. They had wanted to serve their time and go home. I forged ties with some. Many worked in nearby farms and factories during their imprisonment, and later, after being repatriated to Germany, returned to the States for good to marry local American girls. Some of them, realizing I was Jewish, even expressed remorse and said how bad they felt for what happened to my family and other Jews in Germany.

I thought my duties might change when the replacement commander arrived, but any illusions were quickly dispelled. He wanted no part of running a POW camp. He said, "Listen, you and I will get along very well. Just don't bother me, and I won't bother you. After service on the front line for three years, all I want now is peace and quiet. Understood?!" I hardly ever saw him. And, for all intents and purposes, I kept running the camp, with my ability to talk my way out of actual work helping to keep things to my liking. One time, an officer tried to order me to stand watch in the guard towers. Instead of saying, "Yes, sir," which is the preferred army response, I used my own version. It was called, "You got a choice."

"If you want me to stand in the guard towers, I'm not going to be in the POW camp doing the work I was assigned for," I said to the officer. "But you got a choice. Put me up there, and when I get off, I'll go to sleep." He didn't like my argument, but it worked.

I continually tempted fate at Camp Claiborne with my conduct, but I couldn't help myself. I needed to find ways to keep myself interested, and because I spoke the language of the POWs, I had those Germans at my disposal. One day, I was looking at a picture of General Dwight Eisenhower and noticed the general's jacket, which was essentially a single-breasted suit jacket, cut at waist length with two pockets at the chest. No one else in camp had one, not even the officers. Of course, that might have had to do with the fact that it was against regulations to wear one. But what did I care? It was sharp. I *had* to have one. So I showed the picture to a German POW who was a tailor and asked if he would craft my own personal Ike jacket.

The prisoner agreed, and he designed a flawless copy. I wore it around camp proudly. Still, I knew it was only a matter of time until the commander confronted me. When the time came, I was ready.

"Where did you get the jacket?" he demanded to know.

"Why, what's the matter?" I asked.

"This is not army issue," he said. "You're not allowed to have the jacket."

"Well, tell Eisenhower. He's got one," I replied.

He glared at me for a moment, but hard as he tried, he either could not think of a retort or decided I wasn't worth the aggravation. He let out a groan and stormed off. The Eisenhower jacket remained mine for the rest of my tenure at Camp Claiborne.

I didn't escape army duty unscathed as far as facing anti-Jewish sentiment, but antiforeigner sentiment was more prevalent. Fellow soldiers made fun of my accent (more so before I took over as commandant, of course). I tried to pawn it off as a Brooklyn accent, but they weren't buying it. "No way," one GI said to me, "that ain't no Brooklynese." They also called me a "ref," a vicious and derogatory term for refugee.

Still, the antisemitism was there at the time, though I experienced it more deeply during my time off. One time I visited a friend in Baltimore and we decided to take a ride to a Maryland beach. When we arrived, there was a big banner, about 30 feet by 6 feet. It read, "No Jews allowed on this beach." I wondered how free a country it could be if people were thinking like this. Did Americans really understand democracy and freedom? I suppose it was a lesson similar to what black soldiers felt in World War II, Korea, and Vietnam, when they were good enough to fight for their country but still had to sit on the back of the bus and could not drink from the same water fountains when they returned home.

At Camp Claiborne, however, any interest from other GIs in my being Jewish tended to be more out of curiosity. I still recall one of the more fascinating soldiers I met at Camp Claiborne. He was as "country" as it got. He was from Kentucky and never owned a pair of shoes until joining the army. In fact, during our ten-mile hikes, he was permitted to remove the shoes and walk barefoot because they made his feet bleed.

The most memorable thing about him is one of those stories you often hear but would never believe unless it happened to you personally. One day, I mentioned to him that I was Jewish.

"But you don't have horns!" he exclaimed. "I thought all Jews have horns."

The myth about Jews and horns comes from a mistranslation of the Bible from the original Hebrew. The Bible said that when Moses came down from Mount Sinai for the second time with the tablets of God's laws, he glowed with divine light and emitted rays. The words "emitted rays" were taken in one old translation to mean "horns," and the image stuck when Michelangelo sculpted his statue of Moses with horns. I didn't go into that level of detail for the Kentucky soldier, of course, but I assured him that Jews are hornless. I didn't take his naïveté personally.

Among my duties at Camp Claiborne were reading, censoring, and editing the camp newspaper, which was written in German by the prisoners. Amid the drudgery, it struck me that if we wanted the POWs to learn English, it would be helpful if I inserted the English translation beneath each German line. Thus was born our POW camp's first German English newspaper, and this innovation may have been copied in other camps, too.

I still have copies of some of these camp newspapers. In a November 1945 edition, a prisoner wrote how Germans could learn from the four freedoms invoked by President Franklin Roosevelt in his famous 1941 speech: freedom of speech and expression, freedom of worship, freedom from want, and freedom from fear. Another article talked about how the Continental Army needed "*ein Fuehrer*" to step up during the American Revolution. That *Fuehrer* was George Washington. Relax, the prisoner was not equating Washington to Hitler. The POW was using the words "*ein Fuehrer*" in a generic sense, meaning "one leader."

My efforts with the newspaper earned me a promotion to the exalted rank of private first class, and an extra $5 a month in pay, putting me well on the way to millionaire status. Well, by the year 2150, anyway.

ʘ

My tenure at Camp Claiborne ended in January 1946 when I was told that my efforts had earned yet another promotion, to sergeant, and I was ordered to report to the mysterious-sounding Special Projects Center at Fort Eustis, Virginia. Upon arrival, I discovered this center was unlike any army post I had seen before. Nearly everyone besides me was an officer above the rank of major. But these American officers resembled army material less than I did. They didn't know how to wear a uniform, salute, or even how to properly address an enlisted man like me.

As it turned out, I was now part of the Intellectual Diversion Program. The officers at Fort Eustis may have been military misfits, but they were actually a collection of high-powered minds: professors from top universities such as Harvard, Yale, and Princeton specializing in areas like law, government, political science, and economics.

Now that the war was over, the US government wanted to keep occupied Germany from repeating history and sliding off the path of democracy, as it did when Hitler took power in the early 1930s. The goal was to have these professors devise a denazification program to teach about the workings of the American political and economic system. The professors would then give crash courses to other soldiers, who would be the actual instructors and teach the curriculum to specially selected POWs. Upon being sent home, these reeducated prisoners would assume local government positions in the US-occupied zone.

I was selected to be one of the instructors along with a couple of other enlisted men. All of us—the professors and the instructors—were treated like royalty by the army, eating together in the mess hall and getting as fine a culinary fare as the army could offer.

The professors worked at an intense pace. There was little time, and we had much to learn. There was no such thing as taking off for the weekends. The learning sessions were dry, especially considering politics and economics were hardly my natural subjects, but we persisted.

I enjoyed the opportunity to learn from these professors. They were good teachers and companions, and I found it pleasurable talking with them. More than once, a professor offered to take care of me if I wanted attend his university after the war. I never took any of them up on the offer because of the cost of college.

One professor's job was to give me a rapid-fire course on public speaking. This course helped more than any of the others, even up to today, helping me overcome stage fright. The professors usually had little in the way of a sense of humor, but I still remember this guy's attempt at a joke.

"You're lucky to face a captive audience," he deadpanned.

Oy vey, I thought to myself. Thanks for the tip.

I ended up giving a series of lectures to the POWs over eight weeks on American democracy. Despite the lesson I received in public speaking, it was daunting to stand alone in front of a large group of prisoners for the first time. For one thing, while there were guards outside the door, I wasn't allowed to carry as much as a sidearm, because it would have been easy for the prisoners to overpower me and seize my weapon. I was genuinely scared and the POWs could sense it. And with my, shall we say, classic Jewish nose, they had no doubt of my ethnicity. "No damn Jew is going to tell me anything!" a POW called out during one of the classes.

But while there was antisemitism, it was not prevalent when it came to the POWs speaking to me one on one. Also, from my discussions with them, it was clear they generally were not aware of the Holocaust. How could they be? They had been fighting on the Western Front, Italy, or Africa, not manning the concentration camps.

One thing that I had known beforehand is that they needed the instruction that we would be providing in one particular area—how a person in authority should treat others. I remember as a child in Germany how even the garbage man would yell at you if he thought you were causing trouble. The concept of respect was foreign to them.

As at Camp Claiborne, I became friendly with a few POWs and actually felt sorry for them. They would write to their parents and their girlfriends, asking how conditions were in Germany, and the letters they received back worried them. Food was scarce. Allied bombings had destroyed many of their families' homes, let alone leaving entire sections of cities in rubble.

A part of my duties was to assist POWs with their personal problems. They would often ask how they would find a place to live. I listened, but there wasn't anything helpful I could say. After returning home to Germany, a handful contacted me through letters, giving their own accounts of the destruction that war had wreaked upon their country and their houses. Hunger was widespread and some asked if I would ship food parcels. I never did. In fact, I never corresponded with any of the ex-POWs for long. I might have sympathized to a degree with the nicer ones, but I wasn't interested in a longstanding friendship.

It was shortly after I arrived at Fort Eustis that Fred went from being a nickname to my official name. Initially, it appeared that my duties would involve an assignment in Germany, and my commanding officer said I could not go as a member of the army without US citizenship. Therefore, on February 20, 1946, I traveled to the US District Court in Norfolk, Virginia, for army-expedited naturalization proceedings. During the naturalization, the judge said, "Don't you want to change your name from Fritz? Why don't you call yourself Fred or Alfred?" So I went with Fred, which is what I was called in school anyway, and dropped my middle name of Bernhard. Of course, that meant nothing to my mother and father. The name Fred never came out of their mouths. It didn't mean much to many of my fellow soldiers, either, who got a kick out of calling me Fritz.

As the lectures to POWs drew to a close, my fellow instructors and I were sent to New York for the next leg of the mission. From April 4 to May 7, 1946, we would conduct polling of the POWs to determine our program's effectiveness.

It was here that I resided in my finest army housing yet. I was supposed to stay in quarters on Governor's Island in New York Harbor, but, I told my commander, why should I stay there when my parents lived on 111th Street? To my surprise, he agreed. My parents were thrilled. However, my father could only wonder about the US military. Seeing me picked up and returned by staff car, he would shake his head and groan every time. He would say things like, "This could never happen in the German army," and my personal favorite, "I can't understand how America could win the war."

Our offices initially were in the Wall Street area, where I met an associate of George Gallup. Gallup polls had gained fame in 1936 for predicting Roosevelt's victory over Alf Landon in the presidential election when a more prestigious poll predicted otherwise. Here in 1946, Gallup's organization was working for the US government, having been requested to devise a poll to measure whether our denazification program had succeeded. I joined my Intellectual Diversion comrades in giving reports on our sessions with the POWs, from which he devised poll questions. We told the Gallup associate that the poll needed to be short and to the point, because otherwise the prisoners would run out of patience. A week later, after numerous conferences, a fourteen-question poll had been devised in English. We translated it into German, and the final version was simply titled, in both languages across the top, "What Is Your Opinion—*Was Ist Ihre Meinung?*" Prisoners were given the poll at a nearby base before being shipped back across the Atlantic.

I was hopeful that the poll would demonstrate that POWs had gained some appreciation for America after we treated them so well in our camps. I was no longer the smart-mouthed guy who earned KP all the time with his antics. I had been given real responsibility and, finally, was gung ho again about my army role, let alone that the military had spent large sums on the Intellectual Diversion Program and hoped to hear that these efforts were paying off. My fellow instructors and I worked around the clock to translate the responses from German to English. As we did our work, we encountered a number of chilling remarks.

For example, one poll question asked: "What impressed you as most important while you were interned as a prisoner of war in America?"

A POW replied: "The Americans are an uncultivated and uncultured people who are allowing the hoodlum Jews to lead them and cheat them."

One question pertained to the effectiveness of materials shown to the POWs regarding the true nature of the concentration camps. Even though the question was multiple choice, one POW wrote in, "Those who are in the concentration camps only got what they rightly deserved."

Upon finishing our translations, we tabulated the results. Personally disturbing were results regarding the Jews. One-third said that materials handed out that described what happened in the concentration camps were American propaganda. Then there was another question that asked: "Do you think that the Jews are the cause of Germany's misfortune?" The poll gave three possible answers: fully, partially, and no. Fifty percent selected partially. I wrote the following in my evaluation report to my commanding officer in May 1946:

> We may have been successful in reeducating them in many things, but race prejudice does not seem to be one of them. We must remember that [they] are returning home with these ideas in their minds and are on the verge of rebuilding Germany economically as well as socially. If they start out fresh again, believing this . . . all our work here has failed.

Overall, the results were not much better. The Germans, it seemed, hadn't learned much at all, or if they had, simply weren't interested in what we'd taught. They indicated some interest in democracy, and they were impressed with America's freedom of speech and of the press. But they saw little reason for Germany to bear any war guilt. Here is the summary that I wrote at the end of my evaluation report:

> In my opinion, all the programs that were given to them here in the United States were not too successful. The roots of Nazism were planted too deep in most of them, and although they might have given the appearance of little lambs on the outside, they were but little changed on the inside. Many of them were opportunists and can not be depended upon. They are going back to Germany almost . . . the same as they left it. Only a very few of them changed through our influence. Those are mostly the older ones. I am sure that we have tried everything to make human and civilized beings out of them. If we have failed in this I am sure it isn't our fault. Only time can tell us the results.

My God, how disappointed I was. We tried so hard to be good to them, to explain how much better life would be if they would adopt at least some of our beliefs. We were young guys who truly believed in our efforts. You cannot stand in front of people and talk to them unless somewhere deep inside you feel you are doing the right thing.

At the base, we put the POWs through one final interrogation. Afterward, they were put on ships for their departure. Yet many prisoners were not repatriated to Germany. They were sent to other countries such as France and Great Britain, where they were used as forced labor for several years. We heard that the real bad guys—those who felt Germany was better off with Hitler and without Jews—were sent to the Soviet Union, where they were transported to Siberian labor camps and never heard from again.

Because of our exemplary work in the Intellectual Diversion Program, we were told that we could serve our remaining time in the army at the location of our choice. I requested to stay with my parents in New York. But for some reason, the army didn't go for it a second time. Instead, I wound up at Fort Bliss, outside of El Paso, Texas.

When I arrived early in the summer of 1946, I was struck by the quarters that I received. They were even nicer than my parents' house. I was assigned to an annex of the William Beaumont Army Hospital where the doctors and nurses were housed. I had a private room and bath and access to a swimming pool.

The security at the compound was also as high as could be. Soon, I found out why.

CR

On Germany's Baltic coast is a fishing village named Peenemünde. It was there that a scientist named Wernher von Braun established a rocket research installation and led testing efforts. Toward the end of the war, Germany's leading scientists, engineers, and mathematicians eventually succeeded in one of Hitler's pet projects, building the infamous V-2 rockets that flew hundreds of miles to terrorize London. In what the US government labeled Operation Paperclip, after the end of the war, the military worked with von Braun to engineer the surrender of his rocket team—including 500 leading scientists—along with their plans and test vehicles. Despite his Nazi credentials, including an honorary rank in the SS presented by its chief, Heinrich Himmler, von Braun was sent to Fort Bliss to work on the new US rocket program.

Von Braun eventually would become a famed spokesman for the US space program and architect of the Saturn V rocket that sent Americans to the moon. To me, he would become known as my special assignment. For several months, I was among a handful of soldiers assigned to accompany him and his fellow scientists as translator and intermediary.

But even though I was just a young kid, unlike the other soldiers who were older than me and had training in fields such as engineering and aeronautics, von Braun gravitated toward me. I can only assume that I had earned this assignment by demonstrating some level of intelligence in the Intellectual Diversion Program, working with ivory tower professors and teaching the lessons they had devised to groups of prisoners. When he saw I could understand a good bit of what he was working on, let alone that I came from the same country, he would spend time with me and take pains to explain his work.

Accompany is a mild way to describe what I was doing. I was with him constantly. I followed him all around camp. If he and the others wanted to eat at a good restaurant or find somewhere to enjoy a beer in El Paso, or if they wanted to venture across the border to Juárez, Mexico, I came along. Fortunately, he was a gentleman through and through. He was a *Junker,* a member of Germany's nobility. So when I say gentleman, I mean his manners were like those of an English lord. He treated people very respectfully, including Jews. If his attitude toward Jews were otherwise, it would have been clear, because many of the army personnel who were engineers were Jewish. He was a conversationalist who would not hog the discussion and would interact with you. He and the fellow scientists weren't prisoners; they even received a paycheck. But with guys like me following them around, they half-jokingly called themselves POPs: prisoners of peace.

I enjoyed my time with von Braun, and I feel certain he did likewise. I have a souvenir of our time together—a photo of him at White Sands, New Mexico. His message to me on the back (translated from the German) read, "*Herr* Behrend, for a remembrance of the beautiful and productive days in Ft. Bliss and White Sands. —Prof. Dr. Wernher v. Braun."

Serving as the shadow of von Braun and other scientists wasn't my only job. I also translated letters and documents between von Braun and top German leaders that had been seized. These documents related to Peenemünde, discussing matters such as sites to launch the V-2s bound for England and where rocket materials could be obtained. Many of these documents were letters that circulated among top German leadership. Names on those letters included Goebbels and Rudolf Hess. Some may have been addressed to Hermann Göring and perhaps Hitler himself. Believe it or not, for a guy who was only 19 or so at the time, the name of Hitler was not an attention grabber, so I do not recall for certain.

Over the years, von Braun said he was not an ardent Nazi. Still, controversy would follow him because his V-2 rockets were constructed at a forced labor camp in Mittelwerk, where many prisoners were tortured and killed (he denied seeing the worst of this, though conceding in historical accounts that by 1944 he was aware that many prisoners died).

So was von Braun a true Nazi? My feeling is that he had no political bent and was willing to work with any government willing to let him pursue his research, regardless of whether it was America or Hitler's Reich, and regardless of moral issues. He and his fellow scientists had their minds in the sky. They were idealists who cared only for their work, not politics.

In fact, speaking of a lack of concern for politics, I learned from spending time with these scientists that the best of their colleagues went to the Soviet Union. The Russians' offer of grand research facilities to scientists willing to work on their rocket program proved a more attractive offer. The scientists' words proved to be more than rumor when the Soviets won the space race and launched Sputnik into orbit in 1957.

One day in von Braun's office in Fort Bliss, I noticed a blueprint on his wall of an object that resembled a bicycle wheel—a round shape, but with just a couple of spokes. I asked him what it was. He explained it was a station that someday would travel in the Earth's orbit and be a place where humans would live and conduct research. He added that he believed it would be constructed in the near future. I thought he was crazy and told him point blank.

Looking back, of course, I realize von Braun was far from crazy. The diagram looked astonishingly like the International Space Station of today. In March 1952, *Collier's* magazine began a series detailing von Braun's visions of space flight that captured America's imagination. The magazine included an illustration much like the one I had seen hanging in his office six years earlier.

The most fascinating of my army days were spent at White Sands Proving Ground, where we were transported weekly to test fire rockets from the batch of 100 or so that the Americans had seized at Peenemünde. The Germans were so far advanced that American engineers never figured out how to duplicate what the Germans had devised: a heat shield that would not melt or burn up. It would be years until American engineers came up with the tiles that prevent rockets and space shuttles from burning up upon reentry into the Earth's atmosphere.

I always looked forward to my trips to White Sands. Here was a kid who had never been on an airplane, and suddenly I was watching rockets being launched into the atmosphere. I've got plenty of pictures: rockets going up, rockets ready for launch at the gantry crane . . . you name it, I've got the pictures. That's even though nobody was supposed to have a camera, not even the members of Congress and other VIPs who were regularly paraded through and watched launches from a small viewing stand.

The army wined and dined congressional members to ensure the dollars kept flowing, and von Braun would give them a well-rehearsed talk on the program's potential. Enlisted personnel were supposed to remain inside a cement blockhouse, with walls some nine or ten feet thick, when the rockets were fired. Sirens would signal when a launch was coming and it was time to retreat inside. But you could barely see anything through the tiny window slits inside the blockhouse. That didn't work for me. So I stayed outside with my camera.

I wet my pants more than once. I didn't know if I was more scared of the rockets coming down or the rattlesnakes right beside me. I would hide behind large sand dunes and snap pictures. But when the rockets returned to Earth, believe me, I was flat on my stomach. As long as they went up into a trajectory, things were fine and they landed harmlessly in the desert. But if they started doing the crazy dance, as we called it, moving this way and that, you ran for your life. One rocket went up about 100 feet, started the crazy dance, and landed not 50 feet away from me, exploding in a fireball. With my face pressed into the sand, I could hear and feel the whoosh of metal screaming over my head in all directions. I never got that close again, but I continued to stay outside and take my pictures. Every once in a while, after a test launch, a congressman would see me with a camera.

"Hey, soldier, by any chance did you take pictures?"

"Sure, I took pictures," I'd reply.

"Would you have any? We'll give you our names and addresses. Could you send them to me?"

"*Surrre!*"

Did I make money off this? Do you think my parents raised a fool? I was always happy to help . . . for a small gratuity.

Recently, I came across a 1947 *New York Times* article headlined, "Wild V-2 Rocket 'Invades' Mexico," the subject of which is self-explanatory. I laughed aloud as I read the story. Two other V-2 rocket "invasions" had occurred when I was stationed in Fort Bliss the year before. It wasn't hard to figure out where they had gone down. White Sands is a relatively short distance from the Rio Grande. If the rocket went the wrong direction and headed for the river, you knew where it was landing. At least to my knowledge, these errant missiles never triggered an international crisis.

Because of my youth, I did not fully comprehend the historical nature of what I was witnessing when I accompanied von Braun, at least not until the end of our journey together. It was only years later, after the United States had placed a man on the moon, launched the Space Shuttle program, and built the International Space Station, that I realized the full significance of my moment in time with von Braun. In July 2011, after the shuttle's final mission, I swelled with pride perhaps more than ever before, knowing I had been there at the beginning of the US space program.

In October 2014, I swelled with pride even more when I realized I had been there for one of mankind's greatest achievements—the mission that gave humanity its first ever pictures from outer space.

The photos were taken on October 24, 1946, just a bit more than a month before my army tenure ended. Grainy black-and-white photos, taken every 1½ seconds by a 35-millimeter motion picture camera aboard the V-2, were taken from an altitude as high as 65 miles, showing the profile of the Earth against the blackness of space for the first time. *Air & Space Magazine* published a story in 2006 mentioning some other enlisted man my age, Fred Rulli, who got to see the scientists "jumping up and down like kids" when they found the steel cassette containing the film unharmed, then going completely nuts later at the launch site when the photos were projected on a screen for the first time.

Where was I at the time? Clearly, I was in White Sands, because I was there every time a V-2 rocket was fired. But why von Braun never bothered to mention this little bit of history, I'll never know. It was only by chance, when my coauthor Larry Hanover noticed stories about the event on its 68th anniversary, that I finally learned that my days with von Braun, in the scientist's words, had been more "beautiful and productive" than I realized.

C&3

Around this time, I did what proved to be the favor of a lifetime for an old friend from Lüdenscheid named Kurt Simon. If you recall, earlier I mentioned that my parents had to revamp the entire inventory of their store when a competitor moved into town. The former department store bought out by this new competitor was known as S. Simon and had been owned by Kurt's parents. His parents moved to Philadelphia and became friends with my parents, and they stayed in touch with one another. His parents had been millionaires in Germany, but like mine, were nearly penniless by the time they escaped Germany.

As for Kurt, I thought of him when I heard the Army needed translators for the upcoming war crimes trials in Nuremberg, Germany. When I ran into him later, he informed me with great excitement that the job had come through. He would receive his military discharge and a salary of $7,500 plus expenses to serve in a civilian capacity. This was an extraordinary sum at a time when people considered themselves lucky to be making $12 a week.

A few weeks after Kurt headed for Nuremberg, around the Thanksgiving holiday (and my twentieth birthday), I was called to headquarters to meet with a colonel who asked if I, too, would be interested in being a translator at the war crimes trials. I would have to reenlist for three years, but I would receive a promotion to first lieutenant as a reward. I said no. Then he upped the ante, offering the rank of captain.

Now I liked the idea of having a role as Nazis went on trial. But between "dangerous duty" pay, living expenses, and other considerations, as a sergeant, I was already making the equivalent of a lieutenant colonel's salary. The army might have thought this was critical duty in one of the biggest courtroom dramas in history (OK, the army was right about that one, it turns out), but I told the colonel he would have to offer me the same deal as Kurt if he wanted my services: I wanted the money *and* my discharge. Take a pay cut to go to Nuremberg and reenlist for three years just because the army asked nicely? Forget it! The colonel looked at me as if I was crazy, but I turned down the offer and left his office.

Little did I realize that I had ticked off more than just this one colonel. This time, my reward wouldn't be peeling a roomful of potatoes.

It was about a week later, on December 1, 1946, when I received an order to report to the base hospital for a physical. Within hours, this ho-hum ordeal turned into an unexpected drama with a shocking climax—an officer handing me my discharge papers, $300 in cash, and a warning that I had better get off base in 24 hours if I didn't want to land in jail.

Though initially caught by surprise, once the news sunk in, I was able to calm down quickly. After all, this was my fondest wish—a return home to my parents. The base still had a plane, and the pilot was a friend of mine, so I figured I could start on my way without too much difficulty. I drove to the airport and asked him when he'd be flying north.

He looked at me in disbelief and told me to get away from him. Word clearly had spread that I was a pariah, although no one knew why.

"What the hell did you do to them?" he asked, at which point I realized that the army had considered reporting to Nuremberg as more of an order than a friendly request.

He settled down and agreed to help. Finally, we figured out that I could stow away on a plane bound for Chicago the next day, and then make my way home from there. So that's what I did. In the darkness of night, I sneaked out of my quarters. Then I squeezed through a hatch in the plane, scrunching my belongings through the opening as well. I bided my time until the light of morning. After a few hours had passed, the pilot arrived, I felt the vibration of a whirring propeller, and we were aloft. I was on my way to Chicago.

Geography, however, was never my strong suit. When I arrived, my swollen sense of pride quickly deflated as I came to a realization. I was barely any closer to home than I'd been before.

It also dawned on me that I'd never been asked to turn in a special pass that I'd carried throughout my time at Fort Bliss, which said I was on a mission for the War Department and was to be given all assistance in the performance of my duties. At that moment, it turned out there was a commercial flight to New York waiting on the runway. After I explained I was on an urgent mission and showed my pass, the plane was stopped from taking off and a boarding platform was wheeled over. Because the plane was fully loaded, a passenger would have to be taken off to make room for me. It turned out to be an army major, bedecked with combat ribbons. He was carrying a duffel bag over his shoulder and he was steaming.

He took one look at me and growled, "You mean to tell me that I had to give up my seat for *you*?"

I looked him straight in the eye and didn't miss a beat with my reply: "Sorry, sir, but as you must know, war is hell."

This leg of the flight was far more comfortable than the first. Six hours later, I landed at LaGuardia Airport and boarded a taxi for my parents' home in New York.

CHAPTER 7

Finding My Way in New York

When my family first arrived in New York shortly before Pearl Harbor, America may have been a melting pot, but no one had turned the burners on the stove very high. Attitudes toward Jews were only melting a little here and there. Many hotels and vacation resorts excluded Jews, so if you wanted to escape the summer heat, you went to the Borscht Belt hotels in the Catskills, including Grossinger's, Kutsher's, and my little-remembered postwar spot, the Takanassee Hotel.

As far as getting an education, there weren't many places for Jews to go before and after the United States entered the war. Even Columbia University, in a Morningside Heights neighborhood where thousands of Jews like me lived within walking distance, joined Ivy League sisters like Yale and Harvard in setting strict quotas on Jews. Historian David Oshinsky, writing in his book *Polio: An American Story*, pointed out that vaccine inventor Jonas Salk had to go to New York University for medical school because it was one of the few places accepting Jews. Oshinsky noted that in 1935, Yale accepted 76 of 501 applicants overall, but only 5 of 200 of the Jewish ones. "Never admit more than five Jews, take only two Italian Catholics, and take no blacks at all," its dean instructed.

But more than half a million Jews fought for their country in World War II, a contribution that America could not deny. The horrors of the concentration camps turned people's attitudes, too. The official kind of antisemitism that led to Roosevelt turning away the *St. Louis* gave way to Truman recognizing the State of Israel when it was created in 1948. The official barriers to Jews were just beginning to fall by the time the army discharged me at the end of 1946. The attitude toward Jews and refugees of any sort, however, could still be intimidating, as many Americans resented anybody different. That meant it was all the more important for those in our German Jewish enclave in upper Manhattan—tens of thousands who were transplanted here family by family, parent by parent, child by child, from our original homeland—to take care of one another so they could make it in an America that could be welcoming and forbidding all at once.

It was in this environment that I had to figure out the next part of my life. In 1944, the year before World War II ended, Congress passed the GI Bill, which among other things provided up to $500 toward college tuition—more than enough to cover the cost at most institutions. Colleges, formerly a destination almost exclusively for the wealthy, suddenly were open to ordinary people like me for the first time in history.

Now, I was no Jonas Salk, so I found myself applying to the City College of New York and the other local schools that Jews, out of force of habit, were still attending in droves. But the GI Bill at least gave me hope that I could pursue a college education. That hope didn't last long. In my case, it turns out the GI Bill had become *too* popular to be of any help. Colleges across the country were overwhelmed with returning veterans. All the schools I applied to had the same answer by the time they processed my applications in early 1947. They would love to have me, but I would have to go on a waiting list for two to three years.

I would have been content to wait it out. My father, however, would have none of it. If I couldn't get into college fast enough, I'd have to use my GI Bill money to go to trade school. One Sunday, he came in with the *New York Times* under his arm, told me to sit down next to him, and we looked over the help wanted ads. We took out a piece of paper, drew lines for columns, and sorted the ads by type of profession. Two categories of jobs offered the greatest number of job opportunities. It was a toss-up between auto mechanic and electronics. Not particularly wanting my hands to turn black from grease, I opted for electronics. I wound up going to a technical school called the RCA Institute, where I took an intensive course over 1½ years and left with a certificate that stated I was a fully qualified electronics technician.

Soon I had my very first full-time job, which was to service a new invention on the market that promised the buyer static-free radio reception. It was called an FM tuner. Unfortunately, my impressive-sounding RCA Institute training included no practical training on such a device. The job ended on the first day, with my dismissal possibly connected to when I asked the foreman how to turn the damned thing on. I went through so many jobs over the next several weeks that my father said I must have enrolled in aviation school and received a pilot's license, because all I did was fly from one position to another.

It was the overwhelming number of jobs available and the desire to help veterans of any sort that helped me gain employment despite the prevalent attitude of Americans toward refugees, or "refs" as we were called. The label was as insulting as you could get.

I was called a "ref" almost instantly because of my German accent—just as in my army days—wherever I applied for a job. In my eyes, it was not an antisemitic term, however, because it was an equal opportunity insult. It applied to any European refugee, whether Polish, Hungarian, or some other nationality. We came for refuge, so by definition, we *were* refugees. We understood that label. But to be called a ref meant you were a second-class person. It was as hurtful as the "n" word for a black. Anybody new to this country was discriminated against upon arriving in the United States. It happened to the Italians. It happened to the Irish before them. Americans always look down on immigrants until someone newer comes along and the first wave of immigrants has a second and third generation that begins to assimilate.

Eventually, I found a job and lasted long enough for my "ref" status to seem to fade into the background. It was at a company called Regal Electronics, which manufactured TV chassis. The job was perfectly suited for my "specialized" training (which had plenty to do with electronics but little to do with TVs). The plant was so large that I was there for several weeks before anyone realized I had virtually no idea what I was doing. When my foreman did, I was so firmly established that, instead of giving me the boot, he asked if I'd be willing to start from the bottom up and be trained properly. Soon I was in a production line where I was entrusted to solder together two blue wires. After a few weeks, the total was up to five wires. My future seemed limitless. Within a short time, I didn't have to fake it anymore. A few weeks turned into three years and my fellow workers elected me shop steward of Electrical Workers Union No. 2.

But at the time this was among the most corrupt unions anywhere. I found that out when a dispute arose after Regal decided to cut overtime pay. The employees objected, and the union went to management to negotiate. I sat in and spoke my piece. Nothing was accomplished in the meeting, but afterward, the union rep asked to stay for a few minutes. He proceeded to tell me in the clearest terms to keep my big mouth shut and go along with whatever management decided. Obviously, the union rep was being paid off by management. Further evidence came when I was offered a substantial raise along with regular bonuses on the condition that I, too, go along with whatever management said. But I refused to sell out my fellow workers. Many of them were my friends. They trusted me and I was not going to see their trust misplaced. Management asked me two more times to change my stand. Each time, I turned the offer down.

A few days later, I got a different kind of offer—a blindside punch from someone who could only have been a union goon.

I was heading home for the night from my job with Regal on 127th Street along with a few coworkers. As I crossed the street, I was approached from behind by a tall muscular man. He punched me in the face with brass knuckles and left me unconscious, bleeding profusely in the middle of the street. My friends picked me up, dragged me into a nearby bar, and spread me out on a table, where they applied ice to my face and stopped the bleeding. I was then taken to the emergency room of a nearby hospital, where it was determined that my nose was broken in two places and that I had a large cut over one eye and several cuts on my face, lips, and gums. After receiving numerous stitches, I was cleaned up, bandaged, and sent home. My parents were in a state of shock at my appearance.

Figuring I had been through the worst of it after staying home for two or three days, I reported back for work. I was quickly told that I had been fired for not calling in sick. This, of course, made no sense for several reasons. First, the whole factory knew what had happened. Second, my parents had called to let my supervisor know I had been to the emergency room and would be out while I recovered. I went to the union office the next day to seek assistance in reclaiming my job. Immediately, I understood the union had no intention of helping to reinstall a ref who refused to play ball.

But I wasn't going to give up my first real job without a fight. I was told that I would have a better chance suing the union than Regal, so I decided to pursue that avenue. An acquaintance of mine recommended one of the top lawyers in town, one who specialized in labor and union disputes. I felt like I had stepped into Buckingham Palace as I entered the lawyer's office near the top of the 77-story Chrysler Building, with ornate decorations on the walls and a lovely receptionist sitting in an entry room that just by itself was the size of my parents' entire apartment.

I was finally ushered into the presence of His Holiness, The Lawyer. Squinting at me over his giant desk, he asked a few brief questions about my case. As I began to answer, however, he stopped me before I had scarcely said a word.

"You have an accent," said the lawyer, whose name I will withhold out of an excess of charity. "Where do you come from? Germany?"

"I was born in Germany and immigrated to the USA in 1940," I told him. "My parents and I . . ."

He interrupted before I could go any further.

"Are you one of those Jew refs?" he asked.

Startled, I didn't know what to say. I silently nodded yes.

"Then get the hell out of my office," he said. "I don't deal with refs, especially if they are Jews."

What made it doubly surprising was that the lawyer was Italian, which meant his family probably had not been in America that long. And generally, the Italians I encountered were extremely friendly. If I went to a food store owned by Italians when I was younger, they would give me a cookie or candy and talk kindly. To be treated like this by a man of standing, an educated person, a lawyer, was shocking.

My parents were concerned that they would have trouble finding someone to fix the damage to my already pronounced proboscis due to troubles that "refs" often encountered. We heard many doctors would refuse to treat refugees because they worried about getting paid. But that's exactly why we immigrants learned to rely on each other. While others might let you down, others of your background usually stood resolutely behind you.

The German Jewish community had a real mensch of an ear, nose, and throat doctor who came to my rescue. His name was Dr. Joseph Berberich, who had an office on Park Avenue. We didn't know much about him at the time except that fellow German Jews recommended him highly. His 1969 obituary in the

New York Times says he received his MD at the University of Frankfurt but then became a refugee himself, leaving Germany in 1938 to escape the Nazis for a job in London before immigrating to the United States in 1940 and eventually rising to director of otolaryngology at Madison Avenue Hospital.

My father and I sat in his office and, in German, Berberich greeted me by saying, "How can anyone run around in the world with a hook like yours for a nose?"

I swallowed hard. I had been beaten up enough already, and now here was this older German Jew beating up on me, too. I was so scared that I was ready to wet my pants. I was about to turn around and leave when he put an arm around my shoulder.

"Come sit down," he said. "My conscience won't allow me to let you run around with a nose like that. You might frighten some little children."

He winked at my father, who had accompanied me, and told us to relax. My father explained my tale of woe with the Italian lawyer. The doctor shook his head in disbelief. Then he examined my nose. The conversation continued in German as he spoke to my father.

"There's nothing I can do for your son," he said. "It'll never go back to the way it was. You need a plastic surgeon."

"We don't have that kind of money," my father replied, having seen in the waiting room that Berberich's patients were pretty much what you would expect in a fine Park Avenue office—wealthy socialites.

Berberich said he had a plastic surgeon who was well known, one who had quietly performed a nose job on Margaret Truman, the president's daughter. Berberich had sent over so many customers that he had little doubt that the surgeon, whose name I no longer remember, would do him a favor. Without even asking my father, he picked up the phone and called him.

"I'm sending a patient of mine over with a nose that only you could humanize," Berberich said. "He was attacked by a goon and had his nose broken. You've got to do me a favor and look at him. However, you don't have to give me my usual fee for referring him. This boy does not have any money whatsoever. Anything you can do, just take into consideration they are quite poor."

Berberich said the plastic surgeon could see us right away. He gave us the address, which was just five or six blocks away, and we walked over. Like the lawyer, he was Italian. Unlike the lawyer, he didn't look at me as a ref and was as kind as the man who had sent us there.

"Come on in, Fred," the plastic surgeon said. "Let's have a look at you."

He offered my father something to drink and they talked. My father explained to him that we had escaped from Germany. With the Holocaust fresh in everybody's mind, my father had to say nothing further. The doctor knew exactly what my father meant.

The doctor took several photographs, and then he sat me down.

"I can not only fix your nose, but it'll be better than the one you have now," he said. "You'll look like a handsome man. Girls will run after you."

"But how will we pay?" my father interjected.

"Don't worry, I have good customers," the plastic surgeon responded. "I am recompensed by them. You pay me whatever you feel you can afford."

My father said that wasn't an answer. Not to mention that the doctor had explained that we were looking at a four-day hospital stay.

"Don't you worry," he said. "The wing I work in is named after my father. There'll be no hospital charges. My family will take care of that."

The negotiation from there was fairly simple. The average price of the operation was $500 (close to $5,000 in today's money), but perhaps we could afford $300. "You won't have to pay it all at once," he said. "You'll give me $10 to start, and then $10 a month. And if that's too much, let me know. But there has to be some sort of transaction."

The doctor performed the surgery, and sure enough I became the handsomest man alive—at least the handsomest man under 30 in our 111th Street apartment. At any rate, it was a nose of such grandeur and elegance that I stared at a mirror endlessly to admire the awesome change in my visage. This was truly a Roman nose, fit for a nobleman. With new confidence, I started the search for a new job. Eventually, those immigrant connections through a Jewish organization called the New World Club and its publication known as the *Aufbau* would fuel my professional ascent.

⌘

My father's wisdom in steering me toward electronics shone more strongly as the years passed. If you had a television in the early 1950s, you were suddenly the most popular person in the neighborhood. We certainly couldn't afford one in our house. But this newfangled invention seemed destined to have quite a future. *I Love Lucy, The Milton Berle Show, The Jackie Gleason Show*, and others meant more and more people wanted to buy these boxes with the circular screens, with a whole lot of roof antennas shooting up. What did that mean for me? A whole lot of TVs to fix. I first worked with a chain called Davega as an outside service technician.

The post-World War II days also saw the dawn of air conditioners, as they became affordable for the average person. People were taken with the idea of not having to go to the beach or the Catskills to stay cool in the summer.

Fortunately, a fellow German Jewish immigrant named Werner Nathan needed my help. He had just opened a TV sales and service store on Broadway between 178th and 179th streets and gladly took me on. I knew Werner through Boots and Poles, my favorite offshoot of the New World Club, an immigrant Jewish organization dating to the 1930s. Boots and Poles was established in 1947 when a small group got together around two common interests—hiking (Boots) and skiing (Poles). He was merely one of many connections that helped my life blossom in postwar New York. I stayed with him into the late 1950s before going off on my own to work from home. Eventually I found a store on 78th Street between Broadway and West End Avenue that I rented for $35 a month. It was located opposite the luxurious Apthorp apartment. The store was slightly less impressive. The total area was about 20 by 20 feet. But I brought my television sets there for repairs, and people walking along Broadway could see my sign and the TVs and realize there was actual business taking place there. The years passed and I slowly began to see some profit.

Martin Sommerfeld—now *he* was a Jewish immigrant role model. I give him full credit for launching my career full force. For this, I could thank the *Aufbau*'s intervention. Having repaired air conditioners for Davega, I took notice in 1961 when I saw an ad in the *Aufbau* about an air conditioning business for sale. Sommerfeld was a kind, elderly gentleman who had started out in typewriter sales and service, a business that he had conducted in Germany, and then resumed upon fleeing to the United States.

Now, not many people would think to start selling air conditioners and typewriters in the same sales call, but he saw an opportunity. Whenever he dropped in to repair the typewriters, he'd go to the company president or owner and say, "Listen, it is so hot this summer, let me put in an air conditioner so you can be comfortable." It was a stroke of genius. The hell with the employees, they could sweat. But there was barely a company bigwig who didn't want to be sitting cool in his office. In a 20-story office building, you could sell 50 air conditioners. In an apartment building with the right clientele—professionals with plenty of cash to spare—you could do equally well. The math just took off from there. Over time, Sommerfeld developed a customer base of at least a thousand. His business was popular enough that, unlike me with my simple TV repair gig, he was able to make a good living working from home.

But Sommerfeld was getting older, lifting air conditioner units was getting too strenuous, and he wanted to sell the business. He offered it to me for $5,000. To me, this was a veritable fortune—that translates to $40,000 today. And the risk was considerable. He had no office, tools, or equipment. He was selling his customer base, and there was no guarantee once he sold that they would stay with me.

I explained that while I could come up with the $5,000 if I borrowed from family, it would take me several years to make back the initial investment. So he offered me a deal. He was willing to put in writing that if I had not cleared $5,000 in the first year, he would return my money. Could you imagine anyone today making such an offer? But here again were German Jews taking care of each other, regardless of profession or income. With that offer, I had nothing to lose.

"You've got a deal," I told him.

This was the start of West Side Air Color Enterprises, Inc., the business that would sustain me and my family until my retirement 30 years later.

So how exactly could Sommerfeld feel so confident that I would make back my $5,000 so quickly? He spent that whole year personally introducing me to all of his clients, accompanying me door to door to tell them what a fine repairman I was and vouching for my integrity. With each introduction, he also let the customer know that if this younger whippersnapper didn't come through with the same expertise and professionalism that they had come to expect, they should let him know personally. As a sign of his sincerity, he always left his home phone number.

With Sommerfeld's faithful help, I brought in more than double the purchase price in my first year. No refund was necessary, much to the delight of both buyer and seller.

The business was so successful that I would soon be playing Carnegie Hall, or doing the air conditioner repairman's equivalent by doing service work there. In the bustling heart of New York City, I would be serviceman to the stars—actors, singers, authors, and more. My stores were not only near the luxurious Apthorp apartments but blocks from the famed Ansonia, which was home over the years to an array of opera stars, musicians, and writers. Among my clients were superstar actors Robert Redford and Lauren Bacall, Jackie Onassis (President Kennedy's widow), composer Leonard Bernstein, singers Carly Simon and Yoko Ono, authors Joseph Heller (*Catch-22*) and Phillip Roth, New York City's "master builder" Robert Moses, and more.

One of my favorite customers from the immigrant community was actor Paul Muni, who won the Best Actor Academy Award for *The Story of Louis Pasteur* earlier in his career.

After a few words with him, my accent gave me away and he asked where I came from. Upon briefly explaining my background, he spoke to me in Yiddish, but I had to explain to him that I neither spoke nor understood Yiddish because we only spoke German back in my homeland.

Finally, a bit exasperated, Muni leaned forward, put his face close to mine, and playfully said, "*Und Du bist a Yid* (And you are Jewish)?"

As a bookend to my career, shortly before I sold my business and retired in 1991, I met Roth, best known for books such as *Portnoy's Complaint* and *Goodbye, Columbus* and a Pulitzer Prize winner for fiction. During our conversation—stop me if this sounds familiar—he questioned the nature of my accent. I told him the country of my birth. He immediately wanted to know how I ended up in the United States. He listened with rapt attention as I told the story of the exodus of my family from Germany to Cuba to the Upper West Side. He was so interested that he wound up getting the whole package, including my life in the army and close association with Wernher von Braun, developer of the modern rockets.

I had told him I couldn't meet the tight timeframe he wanted for his air conditioner installation. But at the end of our talk, he agreed to a deal. He had just come out with a new book called *Patrimony: A True Story*. I informed him that in exchange for an autographed copy, I would squeeze him into my overbooked schedule. On the appointed day, my instructions to my employees were explicit. They were to ask him for the book before repairing his air conditioner. When my men returned from the job, they waved the prized book in front of my face. I opened it immediately to make sure it was a signed copy. It was. Right on the inside cover of the book, which I keep in my den to this day, he not only had penned his signature but also a message that showed my life story really had made an impression on him. He wrote, "To Fred, who has more stories to tell than I could ever write in a lifetime."

Perhaps one of my favorite clients, however, was a refugee of little fame but one of great stature. He was a doctor named Gustav Bucky, whom I first met in the early 1950s. He was a diminutive man with kind features and a twinkle in his eye. It took me weeks and years to fully understand who he truly was. Initially, I was sufficiently impressed by just his wife, whose name was Frida Sarsen-Bucky.

He invited me to come upstairs to meet Frida and join them for lunch after our service call resulted in a long conversation that determined he and I had something in common—we both had fled Germany. Never one to turn down a free meal, I accepted this offer. His cheerful and lovely wife was overjoyed to have company as well as someone with whom to schmooze.

During our conversation, Frida asked if I knew that President Roosevelt had owned a small dog. Answering in the affirmative, I even gave her the Scottish terrier's name, Fala. There had been a cute song about Fala played over the radio from time to time some years back, which was written shortly before FDR's death back in 1945. To my surprise, she got up from the table and returned with a 45 RPM record with the song. She handed it to me as a gift, which I still have today. It lists her as having provided the words and music.

But now Dr. Bucky would show he had bigger connections than his presidential songwriting wife. The telephone rang, and upon answering it, Dr. Bucky excused himself from the table. He explained that he had a long-distance telephone chess game with an old school chum who was calling to give him his next move. He reappeared after five minutes to finish lunch. He asked if I had ever heard of his old school friend—Albert Einstein. He was shocked when I told him that had I known this before, I would have asked him to give best regards from the nephew of Grete Behrend, my father's sister, who was a nurse in the Einstein household for many years in Princeton, New Jersey. He could not get over how small the world was.

Dr. Bucky remained a loyal customer for many years, and during one visit I learned that he had landmark accomplishments. He asked if I had ever heard of his name before we met. I answered no. He then explained that if I ever had an X-ray taken, I should look at the name on the plate that went under the X-ray table. He informed me that the Bucky plate was his invention and was used to focus the rays for clean, clear pictures. He also invented the Bucky table, providing a grid on which patients sit. Most impressively to me, he bequeathed all royalties and profits from these inventions to charity and research organizations, as he did not want to enrich himself from the suffering of mankind.

CR

The New World Club, along with its offshoot, Boots and Poles, were central to my life. The *Aufbau*, the New World Club's publication, became that way as well. That connection arose about seven years after I got out of the army, around 1953, when I was walking amid the bustle of Broadway and saw a man about my age, also in his late 20s, approaching from the opposite direction. We passed each other. Then I stopped and looked back because I had a sense that I'd seen his face before. And as I'm stopping and turning around, he's stopping and turning around. We looked at each other quizzically for a short time, and then we started walking back toward each other.

"There's something familiar about you," the man said in a German accent. "I seem to know you. Where do you come from?"

"You've never heard of the place," I replied in my own German accent.

"Try me," he said.

"I come from Lüdenscheid," I responded.

"You're right, never heard of it."

"Well, where do you come from?" I asked him.

"I come from Cologne," the man said.

"I know Cologne, too," I said. "I went to a school in Cologne called the Jawne."

He responded that he had attended the very same school. Suddenly, it dawned on him that we did know each other.

"Oh my God, now I know who you are," he blurted out. "You're that dumb kid that sat in front of me, and every time I copied your answers, they were always wrong."

That's how I renewed my acquaintance with Gerhard "Jerry" Brunell. Jerry, who was a year older than me, left Germany for Belgium in 1938 as a mere 13-year-old. He then had to flee Belgium as the Germans invaded, hitchhiking through France, Spain, and Portugal, before finally obtaining passage from Lisbon to New York.

As you grow older, you learn to pay attention to the significance of these coincidences in your life. Looking back, they seem to have a reason behind them.

Such hardship translated into the warmest of friendships, including the one kindled on the spot with Jerry as well as one with a woman named Karola Siegel, who is far more famous than her given name would let on. If not for that meeting, I would never have wound up on the board of directors of the *Aufbau*. Jerry, it turned out, was destined to become its longtime president.

The *Aufbau*, which loosely translates to "reconstruction" and which I fear is being forgotten as the first generation of refugees dies off, was the essence of the German Jewish social fabric across the globe. It was a reflection of the New World Club, which I had become involved with as soon as I got home from the army. The large majority of all German Jewish immigrants in the city were members.

The German-language weekly newspaper was founded in 1934. It was the voice for those fleeing Nazi terror, but more than that, it was a means of communication among our displaced people. It brought culture to our lives, including famous writers such as Thomas Mann, Hannah Arendt, and others. I ended up serving on its board of directors for 20 years. The *Aufbau*, tucked in a fourth-floor office down the block from my shop on Broadway at 74th Street, had subscribers all over the world; a 1959 *Time* article recollected that we had subscribers in 49 American states as well as 83 foreign countries.

It was during the Holocaust and then after the war, while I was in the army, when the *Aufbau* became the center of our lives. For Jews scattered throughout the world, it became the only method of communication. Because the paper by that time was distributed worldwide, including Europe and South America, it transformed into a vehicle to search for loved ones. There were pages and pages of advertisements with the headline *"Es Wird Gesucht . . ."* (We are looking for). They would contain the name of the family or the person for whom they were searching and his or her last known address. Oftentimes, answers would funnel back to the *Aufbau* and long-sought reunions would take place. Families found their children, brothers, sisters, aunts, and uncles in all corners of the Earth. According to JewishGen, a nonprofit organization affiliated with the Museum of Jewish Heritage, from September 1, 1944, through September 27, 1946, the *Aufbau* printed lists of Jewish Holocaust survivors located in Europe, along with a few lists of victims, totaling 33,557 names. The lists are now kept by the US Holocaust Memorial Museum, where they are available today for research.

In later years, because so many German Jews had fled to South America and didn't want their children to marry South American girls, families would place ads in the paper saying they were looking for a suitable partner in marriage for their sons and daughters. Although many refugees in South America had fared well, starting anew in business or manufacturing, they wanted their children to marry into the Jewish religion. Also, congregations in foreign countries would place classifieds seeking rabbis and cantors fluent in their mother tongues.

But aside from the historic nature of the *Aufbau*, it was something that created a connection among us. We didn't completely fit in with Americans, and we certainly didn't fit in with German or Austrian gentiles. While, of course, the second and third generations no longer needed the German language, people like my parents couldn't speak English at all. But even as the population of those who spoke only German diminished, the *Aufbau* retained that strong presence. In our community, when anyone died, preparation of an obituary for the local paper remained an afterthought. The first call was always to the *Aufbau* because it had a higher readership among those who would want to know. This was true even when my wife, Lisa, died in 1991. When the *Aufbau* folded in 2004, it created a true sense of loss for the older German Jews who weren't computer literate and depended on its pages for news.

❦

The New World Club didn't just bring friends into my life. Most important of all, it brought me to my wife, Lisa, an Austrian refugee with whom I spent 30 blessed years.

It began at Lake Oscawana, which, to me, is the most perfect spot on Earth. The annual skiing excursions there of Boots and Poles were an irresistible draw. Many of our immigrant group, it turned out, met their future spouses at this cottage on the lake, not just me.

Lisa Pollak was intelligent, attractive, and fun to be around. She also had a cosmopolitan background that rivaled mine. Her family was from Vienna, Austria. They fled in 1938. Hitler had just annexed Austria, and her parents, having the foresight to leave before it was too late, moved to Panama, which was the only country that would take them. Lisa attended Catholic schools there because they were better than the Panamanian schools. In Panama, she did not have to hide being Jewish, but it was not something you admitted to willingly. As a result of being exposed to so many cultures, she wound up learning many different languages. She spoke Spanish without a German accent. She also spoke Czech (her father was born in Czechoslovakia) and French before eventually picking up English.

In 1950, Lisa decided there was no future for a young European woman in Central America and decided to immigrate to New York. A family friend called on a male relative living in Manhattan, Bill Kunreuter, to arrange an apartment, show her around, and most importantly, ensure she did not fall into the wrong circles. In fact, the word in Panama was that there was a group of young German Jewish people who congregated in a place called Lake Oscawana. The friend strongly advised her to stay away from this sinful place, as there were boys and girls occupying the same house.

Little did they know that Bill was a member of the Oscawana group. So he took her there anyway. And that's how she and I met, on a blind date, in 1955. My friend Walter was dating a young lady named Alice Buchholz who had a girlfriend named Lisa. Alice suggested that he should find a friend for her so they could double date. Lisa and I hit it off from the start.

Lisa did very well for herself professionally and had to help support her parents back in Panama. She was the spender and I was the saver. She won all the money arguments at the time because she made more money than me. Her multilingual background led to a job as office manager in an export-import business and eventually took her to New York, where she worked for a company based in the Empire State Building.

She was high class, dressed impeccably, and could hold her own with anybody in conversation. In fact, one day, the president of Panama happened to be in the Empire State Building. He emerged from the elevator with his security escort and startled everyone when he saw Lisa, gave her a big hug, started conversing excitedly with her in Spanish, and invited her to dinner. It turned out she and his daughter had played together in Panama.

Lisa's bosses were fascinating in their own right. They were in the business of buying and selling ships for oil and grain carriers. They were Orthodox Jews who stopped business for morning, afternoon, and evening prayers. But they had no qualms about providing call girls for the sons of the playboy ship owners who came to negotiate deals with them. Part of Lisa's job was to hire these companions.

Lisa and I dated for six years, and the smart money among our friends was that we would never marry. I had a strong determination never to commit and felt no pressure because I had my mother to take care of me. One day, my mother told me she had canceled our lease and taken a one-room apartment. From then on, I would have to do my own laundry, make my own bed, and cook my own meals. How was a man to exist under such conditions? I quickly caved under the pressure and proposed to Lisa. Practical people that we were, we had a civil ceremony on December 18, 1960, to claim a deduction on that year's income taxes, went back to our respective apartments and jobs, and then married for real with a rabbi under the chuppah (a canopy used at Jewish weddings) on January 22, 1961.

☙

Manfred "Freddy" Westheimer was another friend who met his wife through Boots and Poles. Her name was Karola Siegel. Lisa and I had just returned from our honeymoon in Europe, including some skiing in the Austrian Alps. I was now president of Boots and Poles and eager to be present at our first planning meeting of the season.

Upon entering the room, I saw a little squirt standing on top of a table, expounding on the benefits of one ski area over another and making all the arrangements as if she were the one in charge. She was argumentative and downright annoying. I asked Freddy who this little bombshell was.

"Oh, this is my new girlfriend who I met on the slopes," he replied.

I asked her politely to get down off the table and let the person in charge conduct the meeting. Taking Freddy aside after the meeting, I told him she would never amount to anything and he should stay away from her. He assured me this would be no long-lasting liaison.

But Freddy didn't listen. She would play Freddy like a fisherman casting his baited hook and line into the water, reeling it back in when the poor fish took the bait. Karola, who at this point was going by the name Ruth K. Siegel, is now known as Dr. Ruth Westheimer, America's most famous and beloved sex therapist.

I came around soon enough about Ruthy. All of our hearts were warmed by a ray of sunshine in the form of an adorable daughter Miriam from a previous marriage. We took turns teaching Miriam how to swim, fish, and ride a surfboard. I personally taught Ruth how to water ski. She was a good student. She popped out of the water with the slightest pull of the rope, just like a cork being let go after being held under water.

If not for the *Aufbau,* she might never have met Freddy here or become Dr. Ruth. She recalled in a letter to *The Forward* newspaper in 2004 how she had only come to America in 1956 for a visit and was planning to return to Israel, where she had settled after her escape from the Holocaust. While looking for a room in Washington Heights, she picked up a copy of the *Aufbau* and learned of a scholarship being offered at the New School University for victims of the Holocaust. It was as simple as that. Her life changed forever.

⊂Я

My reunion with Jerry Brunell—and my resulting ties to the *Aufbau*—was just one of the examples of how God's hand has shown itself in my life. Yet there is one other tale that, to me, illustrates the presence of that hand, particularly if we followed his laws and looked after our brethren as called for in the Torah.

It all began with a service call in the 1960s for a lady by the name of Margot Munk. She lived around 95th Street. Her TV had come down with some sort of malaise, and her friends recommended me as an honest and reliable repairman.

Because my customer base was primarily the refugee community, it was natural for conversation to turn to our stories—city of origin, names of relatives, date of escape to freedom, and so on.

I was the first to pose a question, asking the woman what city she came from. She answered that she was born and raised in Cologne. So she asked where I came from.

"I'm certain you've never heard of it," I replied. "I come from Lüdenscheid in Westphalia."

She smiled and said, "This may come as a shock to you, but I know about your city." She then told me how her father, the chief cantor in the Orthodox temple called Glockengasse, had accepted a young boy sometime in the mid-1930s as a boarder. Her father had ascertained that the boy was from a good Jewish family and would make a fine companion for his two children.

"But for the life of me, I cannot recall his name," she said.

I looked at her in utter surprise as a wave of emotion came over me unlike any I had experienced in my entire life.

I took her hand in mine, looked into her eyes, and said, "I am that boy."

We both burst into tears, unable to utter a word for a few moments. Since Kristallnacht in 1938, all I had known about Cantor Baum's family was what I had seen that day. He and his wife had been hauled away by Nazi storm troopers, with their children Margot and Heinz left crying and not knowing what would come next. When my mother sent a driver to pick me up and bring me home, they had been left alone to fend for themselves. Over the years, I had often wondered whether they were still alive.

After catching our breath, Margot and I sat down to ask all the questions that flooded into our minds, and she answered the questions I'd had for more than 25 years. As I suspected, her parents had been killed. The Nazis deported them to Poland, where they were immediately sent to a concentration camp and murdered.

Yet not only had she survived, but her brother Henry (it was changed from Heinz after their escape) had as well. At the time, countries by and large were abandoning the Jews to their fate—what turned out to be Hitler's Final Solution. But after Kristallnacht, the two of them became among the 10,000 children that came via Kindertransport to Great Britain, eventually coming to America and starting their lives anew.

The good Lord travels in mysterious ways. This truly was one of them.

CHAPTER 8

Tales of Other Escapes

Nearly 80 years have passed since Kristallnacht. Yet even now I can visualize the tears and cries for help inside the Baum household in Cologne that fateful November 1938 day, the flames shooting out of the Roonstrasse and Glockengasse synagogues, and the smoldering ashes of prayer books flung on the ground. I can still see the look on my father's face as I awoke where Aunt Grete lived in Hannover after his release from the concentration camp. I can still remember the frantic race to get the documents together in time to board the *Iberia* ocean liner before it departed from Hamburg. I can still feel the sense of relief as the German coastline disappeared from view, mixed with the void in our hearts at leaving our beloved homeland and the anxiety of what our new lives would bring.

But though our lives were changed forever, I gained so much—the chance to have a family living in freedom, the opportunity to rise from poverty to build a business and meet an astounding array of people both ordinary and famous. And it went both ways. America gained a young man who contributed to the war effort in trying to denazify Germans, was there to provide support as the American space program was being born, and became a vibrant part of the Upper West Side's German Jewish community.

But the tale of my exodus to freedom pales compared to the stories of others who escaped the Nazis' clutches and the contributions they made to our society. Here are some of their tales, which I believe bring a fuller perspective to the dangers they faced and the contributions to American society they were able to provide as a result of their miraculous survival, taking them to places from England to Shanghai, from Switzerland to India.

Sadly, although I have a tale of survival for Uncle Otto Oppenheim's family, I don't have one for my uncle himself. My mother's brother, who had moved his family from Hamburg to Copenhagen in the late 1920s to become director for Scandinavian countries for the French grain shipping firm Louis Dreyfus and

Company, committed suicide in March 1940. It happened just before the Germans invaded Denmark and just one year after using every deutsche mark he could spare to arrange my father's release from Sachsenhausen and the safe passage of our three-person family and eight other relatives.

From what I've heard over the years, especially from his daughter Hanna, because of his position as a Jew with influence and power in Denmark and because he had written articles in French and English newspapers attacking the Nazis, the Germans had him targeted for murder. He took his life before the Germans could, as he received word they had discovered the hotel where he was hiding.

Although he did not make it out of the country alive, his wife and children did escape to safety, using the last bit of money he had stashed away for them.

On a cool afternoon in April, less than two weeks after Uncle Otto's suicide, six or seven planes roared over the family's house in Copenhagen. At first, they thought the planes were English, but soon they realized they were from Germany. Warnings came over the radio to darken the windows and not venture outside. Aunt Irene stayed up all night destroying the hundreds of papers and publications my uncle had written. The Danish people and their king would prove kind to the Jews. Citizens helped to hide Jews at great personal danger.

One night, the king's doctor knocked on their door and warned them to get out of Copenhagen. The Germans were coming the next day to round up all the Jews for transport to Theresienstadt and other concentration camps. One of my uncle's coworkers found a fisherman who, for a significant sum, was willing to take Aunt Irene and her three children, Hanna, Ruth, and Walter, and two elderly women to Sweden on his boat. They set out for a small village on the Danish coast to leave at midnight.

They made the short walk in pairs from where they were staying, diving into the bushes as German cars passed by on the roads. Then a tall fisherman helped them into the boat. Hanna's foot landed in a barrel of fish as she got in. That would have been revolting enough itself except for the nauseating odor, which made her ill before they had even started. Finally, they set off for Sweden. Somewhere along the way, the boat halted and dropped anchor. They had rowed into a treacherous minefield and needed to pause to determine a way to slowly navigate past it.

Some 300 Jews were caught in those waters over the next few nights and sent to Theresienstadt, but my aunt and cousins made it to Sweden. They were taken in at a summer camp run by a group of Christian women, where they were eventually given jobs, including Aunt Irene, who became the official one-woman welcoming committee for other Jews fleeing Denmark. After a while, so many Jews arrived that there were no cots left to sleep in, only bathtubs. But after six months, Louis Dreyfus and Company sent money so my relatives could afford to live in an apartment in Guteborg, Sweden. Eventually, my family persuaded them to join us in America. Hanna would later marry a mutual cousin of ours, Curt Jellin, and they lived happily in Manhattan.

ભ્ર

I mentioned earlier about the miraculous escape of the congregants of our synagogue, Ramath Orah, from the clutches of the Nazis in 1941. The tale of the survival of the Jews of Luxembourg can largely be attributed to their leader, Rabbi Robert Serebrenik, who had been the Chief Rabbi of that small nation and whose story I am grateful to be able to retell based on the history from the synagogue website.

In 1940, Luxembourg's population was roughly 400,000, including 4,000 Jews. About half of those Jews had come from Germany during the 1930s, having fled after the Nazis took power. On May 10, 1940, the German army invaded the Netherlands, Belgium, and Luxembourg. On that day, nearly 1,000 Jews fled Luxembourg, and the nations were swiftly overrun.

From the moment of the invasion, Rabbi Serebrenik worked tirelessly to cultivate relations with key German officials, and initially there was little violence against the remaining Luxembourg Jews. But then the Germans developed a plan to expel them on Yom Kippur 1940, with the death camps of the east as their ultimate destination. The rabbi succeeded in having the plan rescinded through his German officer contacts. He also succeeded in organizing clandestine escapes to southern, unoccupied France as well as official convoys from Luxembourg to Lisbon. In fact, from November 1940 through June 1941, Rabbi Serebrenik succeeded in evacuating 2,000 Jews; thus, 3,000 of the 4,000 Jews who had been in Luxembourg on the day of the invasion were now safe.

On March 20, 1941, Rabbi Serebrenik was summoned to Berlin, escorted by two gestapo agents, a clear signal this was no ordinary meeting. This time, he was brought to the office of Adolf Eichmann himself, the architect of the deportations of European Jewry to the death camps.

This is how Rabbi Serebrenik described the meeting in his own words:

> The door opened and I entered into a big office, which I estimated was 15 meters by 15 meters, and at a distance from the door there was a desk, and behind it sat a man wearing civilian clothes. He was dressed elegantly and beautifully. On the door, as far as I remember, there was a sign and Eichmann's name was written on it.

> I approached the desk and then he yelled at me, "Three paces from my body, Jew!" I then noticed that . . . the gestapo men remained standing by the door. I backed up a little bit and then Eichmann started talking to me. "What are you going to do with the Jews in Luxembourg? What are your intentions with respect to them?" I gave him a report and explained to him that my understanding is that the German authorities in Luxembourg are interested in transferring the Jews. In this regard he

said: "This cannot continue like this. How do you expect this emigration to proceed?"

I then explained to him my plan for transferring the Jews. After that he told me: "You are playing a funny game with me. There is no possibility of getting away from the gestapo. Nobody from the authorities can do anything for you. Luxembourg should be *Judenrein* [free of Jews]. You have to find another way to get the Jews out of Luxembourg. You have 11 days to do that. Otherwise, I have already made preparations for the Jews to start working." ["Working" was a euphemism that Eichmann used for deportation to concentration camps and labor camps.]

Rabbi Serebrenik then asked for a few hours to prepare a memorandum on how he proposed to transfer the Jews of Luxembourg to Lisbon. Eichmann told him to come back later that afternoon, which he did. Again, in Rabbi Serebrenik's own words:

When we entered, Eichmann started to yell. . . .

"Now this must end. If you don't do what I say in the time I give you . . . If you don't do what I told you, all the Jews will pay dearly for it."

After that, Eichmann demanded the memo from me. He reviewed it. He demanded changes in connection with the manner in which the Jews are to be transported and with obtaining Spanish and Portuguese visas. In addition, he demanded that I would obtain the dollars (it is unclear whether this was a bribe or dollars to pay for the transportation). He demanded that I will stop sending Jews to southern France and I will be responsible for this to stop. He agreed to the departure to Portugal. I must use my good relationships with the Joint Distribution Committee. He added that he will be informed regarding my obedience to his commands from Luxembourg. He also said that I do not have enough time since he will close all routes soon.

Rabbi Serebrenik could not save them all. But he had negotiated with the devil himself, Eichmann, and many more did escape. Even after all routes were seemingly shut, in the ensuing months, the rabbi found a way to sneak out 250 more Jews (including himself) before the door was closed for good. The rabbi stayed until the end, even though he was almost beaten to death by Nazi thugs in the final few weeks, and left in June 1941. The Nazis spent the next two years demolishing the Great Synagogue of Luxembourg piece by piece, but Rabbi Serebrenik, his wife, and 61 other refugees arrived in New York, and the next year construction began on the former church at 110th and Broadway, which became Ramath Orah. In total, only 670 Luxembourg Jews could not be saved from deportation to extermination camps. All but 42 of them died.

 CR

For the most part, the world turned its eyes away from the plight of the Jews after Kristallnacht. But to me, it is astounding how few today are aware of the life-saving Kindertransports. They were organized primarily by a group of British Quakers. Some 10,000 Jewish children were evacuated to freedom from shortly after Kristallnacht until the beginning of the war in September 1939. Other Kindertransports took smaller numbers of children to safety elsewhere. I have already told the tale of my cousin Henry Oppenheim. He was taken in by New York City's commissioner of utilities before rejoining his parents Hugo and Herta, who came across the Atlantic with my family and eventually settled in New Orleans.

But there is also the tale of my friend of nearly 60 years, Dr. Ruth Westheimer (formerly Karola Ruth Siegel). Like me, she had little sense of what was befalling her homeland. She simply knew that her synagogue had burned down and that classes at her Orthodox girls' school had stopped after Kristallnacht. Her father, Julius, like my father, was arrested and taken away during that fateful night of November 9–10. The policemen were polite but insistent that he come with them. He was herded into a truck and, on November 16, arrived in the Buchenwald concentration camp.

Five weeks later, her mother Irma and her grandmother told Karola that she would board a train for Switzerland. They made her feel better by saying that by doing so, the Nazis would allow her father to come home. She brought a suitcase with clothes, a doll, and chocolates. She was only ten years old when, on January 5, 1939, she waved goodbye to her family at the Frankfurt railroad station, expecting to see them in six months.

"Be good. Study hard. It will be nice in Switzerland. And we will see each other again," her mother said as she hoisted her into her arms for the last time.

Her mother and grandmother ran after the train as it began to move, waving goodbye. But it would be the last time Karola ever saw them. She was among 100 Jewish children from Frankfurt aboard the transport that saved their lives even as it ripped their families apart.

Her father was released from his detention shortly after Karola went to Switzerland, where she lived in an orphanage overlooking Lake Constance, learning to take care of Swiss children within sight of the German shoreline. She kept in touch as much as possible through letters. But a letter from her parents dated September 14, 1941, arriving around Rosh Hashana, proved to be the last. The next letter, on October 29, 1941, was from relatives telling her that her parents and grandmother had been sent away. It turned out they had been deported to the Lodz ghetto in Poland. She later learned that her parents were killed in the gas chambers in Auschwitz; her grandmother's fate was probably the same.

Karola had fantasized about immigrating to Palestine. After the war, not wishing to stay in Switzerland or return to Germany, she chose to go there and work on a kibbutz. It was in Israel where she was persuaded to shed her German past and start using the name Ruth instead of Karola. When guerrilla warfare broke out between Arabs and Jews upon the United Nations adopting a plan to partition Palestine between them, she joined the Haganah underground army, which was the precursor of today's Israeli Defense Forces. Being short of stature, she could get around fairly well in secret and served as a messenger. She was also trained as a sniper. On May 14, 1948, Israel declared independence, but war broke out with all its neighbors intent on its destruction. On June 4, her twentieth birthday, her youth hostel was hit by a bomb, tearing into the walls of the lobby. She was sprayed with shrapnel, leaving her feet severely injured and requiring a lengthy recovery.

But after moving to France to study toward a degree, she would eventually make her way to America and into my ski group in the company of Freddy Westheimer, where she proceeded to annoy me to no end until she and her young daughter Miriam from a previous marriage began to win me over. Ruthy and Freddy married on December 10, 1961, and were together until he passed away in 1997.

CR

John Mann, a dear friend of mine, was yet another Kindertransport survivor. He was able to escape from Mainz, Germany, for England, where he lived in peace for some time. But with the end of the "phony war"—the period of relative calm between Germany's conquest of Poland and the invasion of France—hysteria gripped the island nation. John, and other German and Austrian teens and adults, were declared enemy aliens by Prime Minister Winston Churchill's government and placed in an internment camp. It didn't matter that they were Jewish refugees. The British government subsequently deemed it too dangerous even to keep them on its shores, so they were placed on a prison ship, the *Arandora Star*, alongside Italian detainees for deportation to Canada in the summer of 1940.

"We were loaded with hundreds of Italians on a converted ocean liner," a shipmate named William Rabinowitz wrote in a 2010 article for *The Jewish Magazine* website. "Churchill did not want to take any chances with us. He ordered that barbed wire be strung along the deck, railings and upper structures to be sure and keep us contained."

But a U-boat torpedoed the ship and it sank in the Irish Sea on July 2, 1940. More than 800 lost their lives. John was among the survivors. After 12 hours, he was picked up by a British destroyer. He and other survivors were returned to England and placed on a second ship, the *Dunera*, on July 10 for transport to Canada. Sanitary conditions were appalling and dysentery ran rampant through the ship. Midway through the journey, the ship was redirected to Australia. On its way there, the *Dunera*, too, was torpedoed. Luckily, the torpedo was a dud and did not explode and the ship made it to Sydney, Australia, where he was placed in another internment camp. The voyage and imprisonment of the Jewish refugees was later portrayed in a TV movie called *The Dunera Boys*.

Mann's story diverged from the other internees at that point, however, as he did not remain long in Sydney. After ten days, he was placed back on the same ship and sent to Mumbai, India. There, he was set free and abandoned. He was able to find work in a factory manufacturing specialty tools, climbing his way to a managerial status in a business deemed crucial to the war effort.

Shortly before the December 1941 attack on Pearl Harbor, he decided he wanted to leave India for America, taking advantage of an offer of passage from the Hebrew Immigrant Aid Society. After sailing past Singapore, the ship was caught in a typhoon and had to anchor at Formosa (now Taiwan). From there, the ship went to Kobe, Japan, where he boarded another that sailed to Shanghai. Finally, he was able to sail for Manila and eventually reach San Francisco. He wound up being drafted into the US Navy and served in a construction battalion in the Pacific theater.

In America after the war, he proved his worth. He established a company that fabricated solderless connections for construction, a critical development in the drive toward space exploration.

ॐ

One of my dearest friends was a man named Frank Lewin, born in Breslau, Germany (now Wroclaw, Poland), in 1925. He was a musical genius, a gifted composer who wound up living in Princeton, New Jersey, writing music for film and television, including for a show called *The Defenders*. Like me, he was forced to flee the country after his father was imprisoned in a concentration camp.

He had his bar mitzvah while still in Germany in April 1938, but seven months later, his synagogue was torched during Kristallnacht. His father, unaware of the arrests and pillaging, had been on a business trip selling ladies' hats in the German provinces. Upon his return, a policeman arrived to arrest him. Frank, who had to sleep in the kitchen after an elderly woman moved in upon eviction from her apartment, saw his mother making sandwiches for his father to take with him. During the ordeal, the policeman asked his mother how old Frank was. She told them he was 12, hoping the cutoff for arrest was 13. If so, she guessed right, because the policeman did not take him.

After 40 days in the Buchenwald concentration camp, his father was released, as his mother obtained a visa to immigrate to Shanghai. But they didn't go to the Far East. Instead, American family members provided affidavits and funds, allowing them to get into Cuba, where we became friends. They set sail in March 1939 and were able to embark for the United States in June 1940.

By the way, you might wonder how a place as distant as Shanghai might figure into the survival of Germany's Jews. Shanghai actually was one of the main destinations of fleeing Jews, as, at the outset, you did not even need a visa to enter. Germany had insisted that its ally Japan, which overran the city and much of the rest of China, place any Jewish refugees in detention camps. But Japan refused. At one point, the Jews in Shanghai were ordered into a ghetto. Although this restricted their movement, it was not oppressive, as the Chinese who already lived there did not bother to leave. The Jews lived in as much freedom as one could reasonably ask for. They had little money but made do with charitable help, particularly from the Joint Distribution Committee in New York.

A close friend of ours from Lüdenscheid who lived in a villa near the Zeppelin compound, Erna Levine, made her escape in 1939 to Shanghai across the Trans-Siberian Railway. Tragically, her husband had just died of a heart attack in my father's arms in shul (synagogue). But things worked out well for Erna, a beautiful, slender woman who drew men to her with ease. While in Shanghai, she met a ship's captain. They became friends, and later in the United States, they married. I think it was more a marriage of convenience than love because he wasn't around 90 percent of the time. He was off piloting ships across the Pacific and the China Sea. She lived in a plush house on the Main Line near Philadelphia and never had to work because she was sustained by her generous captain.

CR

In 1944, my parents were among those shown kindness by a group of Quakers who offered an invitation to spend a week's vacation at one of their properties in the Catskills. My parents were introduced to a couple on this vacation who had lived in the city of Hagen not far from Lüdenscheid. Their story was remarkable, and as they had no children and few living relatives, I feel it is an important one to tell.

In Hagen, there was a large industrial complex by the name of *Westfälische Spiralfedern Fabrik*. This factory, established in the mid-1800s by the Stern family, was the largest manufacturer of industrial springs in Germany. It supplied all the springs for both German railroads and large industrial plants worldwide.

When the founder died, the factory became the property of their only child, a daughter named Elizabeth. Her father had wisely entered her into an engineering school from which she graduated with high honors. But no other companies wanted to speak with a woman in a business environment, let alone conduct negotiations with one. Therefore, it became imperative to find a suitable mate and experienced engineer to help run the company. After a lengthy and discreet search, one was found by the name of Iwan Cohn. This Jewish gentleman not only was a mechanical engineer but a pilot; he flew in the First World War with the renowned Baron von Richtofen, better known as the Red Baron. After being shown the industrial complex and introduced to Elizabeth, the marriage was arranged.

But early in 1939, they were offered the proverbial deal they could not refuse. They were approached by the gestapo and advised to sell the company to a party of their choice for a fraction of what it was worth. Faced with the alternative of being arrested and sent to a concentration camp, they submitted to selling on these predatory terms and subsequently fled the country. Elizabeth and her mother went through France and Portugal to find a haven in the United States. Iwan was barely able to make his way to England. With his experience in industry, he was warmly welcomed there and, with the help of Lord Beaverbrook, a high-ranking British official and a renowned press baron, was ordered to build factories for the defense effort. He distinguished himself but was not allowed to leave Great Britain to reunite with his wife and mother-in-law, as his services were deemed too important.

As a result, for four years, Elizabeth was left to care for herself and her mother, moving into a one-bedroom apartment near my parents on the Upper West Side, her wealth now a distant memory. She took whatever jobs she could find. She was offered only the most menial work. She alternately worked as a cleaning woman, cook, or, if she was lucky, office help. One day, a friend who worked for Philadelphia Orchestra conductor Eugene Ormandy found out his cook had just quit and he was looking for a replacement. Because she knew that Elizabeth was an excellent cook and baker, she asked Ormandy to give her a chance. He agreed, and she stayed with him until the end of 1943, when Iwan was finally reunited with her in New York (they soon changed their name from Cohn to Cope).

Their financial situation began to improve quickly, as he was asked to build and run a plant for rubber products. But when the war in Europe came to an end, he was determined to reclaim what was theirs. He put all of his efforts in motion to return to Germany and sue for the return of their factory complex. With the help of influential friends in the United States and England, he was able to obtain transportation back to Germany, where he stayed for about two years.

He pushed his suit through several courts. Finally, he achieved victory and was awarded the property back. The owner at the time, a former high-ranking Nazi, wanted to buy back the property that he had essentially stolen from the couple. Iwan, however, refused to sell it to him at any price. Instead, he put it up for sale on the international market, where a buyer was soon found at a price of several million dollars. The day after the sale, Iwan left Germany, not to return for many years.

Iwan and Elizabeth remained as our closest of friends. So close were our families that I gave eulogies not only at his funeral but at Elizabeth's when she passed away at the age of 96 in 1996.

CR

One final tale that I want to share is about a relative who did not escape but survived despite a horrific ordeal, Marta Arends. Her son Herman, a cousin of my father, made it to America in the mid- to late 1930s and spent his days with his brother-in-law Harry DeJong and their wives in New York. They were running a small business where they made change purses, cigarette cases, and wallets when both were drafted into the army (leaving a certain teenager named Fred Behrend as the only "man" in the shop). Given our background in Germany, where everyone learned to ski as a pastime and a means of getting from place to place, he wound up with the mountain troops in the Italian Alps fighting for the Americans.

As the war dragged on, Herman lost touch with his mother, who was in her 80s. He was convinced she had died in the concentration camps.

As the war was winding down in Europe in May 1945, however, the Red Cross contacted Aunt Grete in England via telegram. It had been sent from a concentration camp that was overrun by the Allies. The telegram read: "Marta found alive in Theresienstadt." Overjoyed, my aunt contacted Herman, who told his captain the news he thought he would never hear. Although Theresienstadt was north of Prague, Czechoslovakia, and their unit was more than 100 miles away in northern Italy, without hesitation, the captain provided a jeep, food, and blankets and told him go to the camp to find his mother.

He drove there and wandered for what felt like hours among the dazed, emaciated survivors, still wearing their prison uniforms, not knowing what to do or where to go. He asked repeatedly if they had seen Marta Arends, to no avail. Nobody knew the name.

Finally, he came up to an elderly woman who was wheeling a cart and asked if she knew his mother. "Yes, if it is the one I'm thinking of," she said, telling Herman to go three blocks in one direction, then one block in another. "You'll see a big pile of potatoes. And there's an old woman there peeling those potatoes."

He followed the route he was given and came upon an old woman in tattered clothing.

"Mother, mother?" he cried out.

She turned around. He hardly recognized her. But it was her.

"Mother, it's me," he said, tears streaming down his face. "It's Herman."

She could not believe it. She shuddered with fright because all she saw was a man in uniform, and men in uniforms had spent the last several years ordering her around and threatening to kill her if she didn't obey. She had given up on ever seeing her son again. When she finally gave him an embrace, it was a tentative one; she was unable to shake off years of traumatic imprisonment in the space of that one moment. He handed her the food and blankets he had brought and returned to his command post.

As soon as he returned, the captain wanted to know if he had found his mother. When Herman replied yes, the captain assembled a convoy of trucks and had them loaded with food and clothing.

"You go with this convoy and take it to Theresienstadt and see that the people get help," ordered the captain.

Herman could not help her leave Germany right away because of the bureaucracy in place in postwar Europe. She was moved to a displaced persons camp in Austria. But from there, he was eventually able to bring her home to New York. She lived with him until the day she died, living past the age of 100.

CHAPTER 9

Germany through an Older Man's Eyes

I have visited Germany perhaps a dozen times since the early 1960s, shortly after Lisa and I married. I have toured places like the Eagle's Nest, one of Adolf Hitler's former lairs, and I have driven through its lush mountainous countrysides, skied down its snow-packed slopes, and toured its various towns. Given the circumstances, you might want to know what thoughts went through my mind during these visits. Did I have the temptation to gloat about having survived to return to the land where the Nazis had driven my family out? Did I feel a sense of vengeance? Was I overwhelmed with sadness?

Actually, the answer is none of the above. Frankly, I was just there for the scenery.

At the time that we boarded the *Iberia* and left Germany in 1939, I was a sheltered 12-year-old whose parents did everything in their power to shield me from the realities of Nazi terror. That's not to say I don't feel anger toward what Hitler and his Nazi thugs did to us and our fellow Jews. But at the same time, I am displaced enough from the facts of the Holocaust that, to a greater degree than many survivors, I can accept that the Germany of World War II is not the Germany of the twenty-first century. I can be a tourist, carrying only my actual luggage—and not emotional baggage—when I visit the country of my youth. I can be an observer, viewing Germany through a lens that many others of my generation cannot.

With that said, however, there were trips that went beyond just being a tourist, ones that generated headlines because of their significance and symbolism. I would like to tell you these headlines were blared across the top of the *New York Times* and gave me, to paraphrase Andy Warhol, my 15 minutes of fame. Unfortunately, that was not the case. They were all published in Germany in newspapers such as the *Westfälische Rundschau, Lüdenscheid Nachrichten*, and Bückeburg's *General Anzeiger*, costing me any bragging rights that I might have

129

received in the United States. I mention these headlines not just because they appeared, however, but because of the importance of their wording.

First, though, let me tell you how this flurry of events developed. It began in August 1989 as I was reading the classifieds in the *Aufbau*. Right among the advertisements from Munich for a Jewish kindergarten teacher and from a "Handsome Modern-Day Hero" seeking an "intelligent, shapely, sensual, and slim woman" was an advertisement stating, "The city of Lüdenscheid . . . is looking for former Jewish citizens to invite." So I wrote to the city official listed as the contact person. As it turned out, nearly 45 years after the end of World War II, in memory of those killed in the concentration camps, the city was now planning to dedicate a plaque on the wall of the building where our temple held services from 1901 to 1936.

I accepted the invitation, as did my old friend Kurt Simon, who had served as an army translator for the war crimes trials in Nuremberg on my recommendation and now lived in Philadelphia. Lisa traveled with me to Lüdenscheid in August 1990. In total, 11 former refugees returned to their native city; in addition, some adult children came to represent parents who had died.

At the ceremony, a rabbi came from Hannover to consecrate the plaque, which noted that 100 Jewish citizens of Lüdenscheid had used the site for prayer. The plaque read, "During the time of the Nazis from 1933–45, they were hunted, tortured, had property confiscated, were chased out, and murdered. This makes it our duty to remember for the future of mankind." There was also an unexpected reward for my travels, a reunion with the one neighborhood Gentile boy whom I got to play with at all as a child. Wolfgang Brinker, who had lived next door, traveled several hours to see me upon reading about the events in Lüdenscheid in the newspaper.

Mayor Jürgen Dietrich was a gracious host at the ceremony, held outside the old three-story building with white concrete walls where my father had once led prayers in a single large room. But the remarkable thing was the friendship that developed between the mayor and me and the train of events that our bond sparked. His kindness translated into a phone call from his office to that of Bückeburg Mayor Helmut Pruel that opened up the gates of the city's usually locked Jewish cemetery when we wanted to visit the graves of my grandparents Gotthelf and Mathilde Behrend.

More importantly, the fact that we hit it off so well resulted in two more trans-Atlantic trips, both of which generated headlines. Just a couple months later, in October 1990, he came to visit my family in New York as he accepted my invitation to show him where my parents and I had settled and made a life after fleeing initially to Cuba.

Exactly one year after that, in October 1991, both Bückeburg and Lüdenscheid would play host to us for additional ceremonies. It turned out to be a wonderful experience made richer because my children Andrew, who was 27, and Evelyn, 23, were able to partake in the festivities with me. They even got mixed up in the newsmaking.

The headlines that followed spoke volumes about the German psyche and how the nation viewed its tainted past. One word stood out in particular: *Versöhnung*. It is German for reconciliation.

The word is so important because it signifies a most fervent desire for many Germans concerning its former Jews. Reconciliation is what the mayor wanted right from the first invitation and what the German people still yearn for today. They want their guilty consciences put to rest and the Holocaust consigned to the past. They want to move on and they want to do it soon, even though in reality, such reconciliation is probably generations away, if possible at all. After all, the Jewish presence in Germany today bears virtually no resemblance to the vibrant community that existed for centuries before Hitler nearly wiped us all out.

The themes of reconciliation and forgiveness kept playing out over and over again during these visits. They first arose during a visit to a Masonic lodge in 1990 at the time of the dedication at our former temple. I had no idea there was a lodge in Lüdenscheid, especially because Hitler banned all such secret societies when he was in power. But during a conversation with the mayor in which I mentioned that I had served as a master Mason with my lodge in the United States, I discovered otherwise.

"Why didn't you tell me before that you were a Mason?" Dietrich said. "I would've arranged for a meeting with all the masons. They would've loved to have you for a guest."

So the mayor called Dr. Gunter Rosenbaum, a dentist who was head of the city lodge, and told him about me. Rosenbaum got very excited. He said he would round up as many Masonic brothers as he could and invite me to their lodge as a guest. About a dozen men showed up for the occasion. He stood up, put his hand out to welcome me as a brother Mason, and said in front of everyone, "I'm extending my hand hoping for forgiveness for the things that happened to you."

The word "forgiveness" was far beyond the boundary of what I could bear.

"I will extend my hand to you in friendship and as a brother Mason, but I don't want it to be interpreted as a handshake of forgiveness, because forgiveness can only come from heaven," I replied.

Fortunately, that word did not appear in newspaper coverage of the dedication. However, the word "reconciliation" did make an appearance. And it kept returning in a bigger way.

It arose again in New York during the visit by the mayor, who was accompanied by the reporter who covered our first visit to Lüdenscheid, Eddie Graefer, and a wealthy friend of the mayor named Wilhelm Moskob. The mayor was thrilled to come to the Upper West Side and understand a bit more about the lives of refugees, not to mention that any tourist would enjoy visiting the big apple. The tour focused in large part on my old neighborhood, including Congregation Ramath Orah, where I recounted the story of the chief rabbi saving the Luxembourg Jews from Eichmann and told how a shofar (ram's horn) donated by my father was still blown there on the Jewish high holidays. I gave him a comprehensive tour of other places around New York, too, including a special West Side Air Color Enterprises edition to show him some of the renowned places that were home to my air conditioners, including the Dakota building (home to Yoko Ono, among many others) along Central Park, Carnegie Hall, and Columbia University.

Somewhere in the conversation, Dietrich talked about his desire for reconciliation. With Graefer taking notes of the conversation, the word wound up in the *Rundschau* in a headline that read: "City Builds a New Bridge of Reconciliation." I was not pleased with the headline, which I saw when the mayor's office mailed me the newspaper upon his return home, although I was fond of the pictures accompanying the article. They showed the mayor, Evelyn, and me standing along the Hudson River, and the mayor and me outside Ramath Orah. It was a good-looking spread and a terrific keepsake. Even though the mayor and I certainly would never agree on everything, he was a good, honest man, and I was eager to build on this new Old World-New World connection in hopes of broadening my hometown's knowledge of what happened to its Jews.

The next visit to Germany would present an opportunity. My thoughts turned to one of the many Judaic artifacts passed down through the generations. Among them was a megillah (Book of Esther), handwritten around 1650 on a yellowed scroll of parchment. Because it had become worn over the centuries, it was no longer kosher, meaning it could not be used for its designated purpose—to be read at the Purim holiday service. But I felt it would be an appropriate gift to present back in Lüdenscheid, telling a story with parallels to the Jewish experience there. The story of Esther revolves around a plot by Haman, a high-ranking minister of King Ahasuerus, to exterminate the Jews of ancient Persia (present-day Iran). The plot is foiled when the king's new queen, Esther, whom Ahasuerus had not known was Jewish, risks her life by going before him to plead for her people's lives. Haman is hung on the very gallows that he built for slaughter.

Dietrich was delighted at the idea and invited us for a ceremony at the city museum for its official acceptance. Lüdenscheid had recently opened the museum and it had a Jewish section. But the museum had practically nothing to display in that section. It consisted of empty shelves and a cabinet. So it turned out that it needed such an item more than I realized. In retrospect, it should not have been too surprising, considering there were only about 50 Jews living in Lüdenscheid at this point.

At the ceremony, Dietrich expressed his gratitude, calling it a homecoming for a scroll that had resided in Lüdenscheid for so many years. "This is a true sign of reconciliation and will lead to a greater mutual understanding," he said.

Yup, he had done it to me again. Sure enough, the word reappeared in the headlines. "*Ein echtes Zeichen für eine Versöhnung*" read the *Westfälischer Rundschau* in large bold type on October 28, 1991, "A True Sign of a Reconciliation."

This really did bug me. The mayor—and by extension, the newspaper—had it wrong. A reconciliation was certainly not what I intended to convey by presenting my megillah. To think that everything was OK between us just because I presented a Purim scroll? That was a bit much.

Listen, I don't begrudge the German people their desire for wanting the Holocaust to be washed away. In fact, they have probably done more than any nation in history to try to atone for the sins of their past. In 1952, the West German government agreed to pay $845 million in restitution to individual Jews and to the State of Israel itself. Many more millions have been disbursed over subsequent decades. The injection of aid for Israel provided an enormous boost for the stability of a new country that was granted independence in 1948 and struggling to get on its feet. I personally received what I recall as a total of $5,000 in compensation for the "loss of education" that I would have received in Germany. I knew many Holocaust victims who refused to accept restitution, calling it "blood money." Although I understood the sentiment, I disagreed with it. It was only right for Germany to provide compensation. My parents accepted the payments, which Germany sent to those who escaped and could prove they were born and raised there. Until the times of their deaths, my parents lived solely on this restitution money. The funds were generous and made life easier after years of struggle.

An offer of dual citizenship was another means of restitution. In 2010, my family was among those invited to Miami by the German consul general. He had obtained names from the Leo Baeck Institute in New York, which studies the history and culture of German Jewry and has some of my family's artifacts and papers. He asked attendees for two things: to give help in locating the records of any Jews that had escaped from Germany and to encourage living family members to accept dual citizenship with Germany. The obvious argument in favor of accepting it was that, with a German passport, you could easily travel to Germany and not have to pass through customs. Dual citizenship also provided the potential for healthcare benefits and higher education at much lower cost (if any), both of which are available to all German citizens and would thus be available to my children and grandchildren. I encouraged Andy and Evelyn to accept, and they are still considering the possibility.

Can America say it has done the same in trying to make amends? Look at what happened to Japanese Americans during World War II. It took decades for the American government to even own up to the fact that it had done anything wrong in placing them in internment camps for the duration of the war. It was not until 1988 that the country agreed to provide $20,000 to each surviving detainee. The United States' history as far as how it treated its Native Americans is equally appalling.

Why did Germany outperform America when it came to restitution, even going so far as to become one of Israel's staunchest allies and trade partners? Guilt. Once the gates of those concentration camps were opened and the gas chambers and mounds of cremated bodies were revealed, there was no denying the evil that this once great nation had wrought. I cannot picture a human without some sense of guilt after witnessing this.

It was rewarding to see Lüdenscheid make a conscious effort to remember its past and try to build a new future based on tolerance and respect. But, of course, there were a variety of feelings as I talked with Evelyn and Andy while walking through the streets in October 1991. A year earlier, I had asked the mayor to show us 10 Paulinenstrasse, the site of the Zeppelin compound where I had lived from 1930 until we fled to Cuba. He didn't know what I was talking about. The compound did not exist anymore. I was upset to be unable to show Lisa where I lived.

So this time, even though the house was gone, I was determined to go and at least show my children whatever I could. It turned out the property now had a church, a hospital, and something called *Kulturhauspark,* or House of Culture Park. All I could do was point to the unfamiliar buildings and the grass, trees, and pond. One remnant still existed—the stone wall that completely surrounded the property and its iron gate. I was able to point to the flight of about 30 concrete steps where I had tried to ride down on the gardener's bicycle and wound up unconscious at the bottom. We took a picture as Andy reenacted the final result of the landing, lying splattered in an unconscious state.

I also showed them where my parents' store once stood. The street had been widened and modernized. There was now a plaza with fountains and stores, replacing the cobblestone streets that existed in the days of the Kaufhaus Robert Stern—the store named for my mother's first husband who died in World War I. As for the three-story building itself, it had been repainted yellow and was now a pet store. Across the street still stood the building where authorities jailed my father after Kristallnacht. There had been a statue dedicated to my mother's first husband, Robert Stern, commemorating that he had been the first Lüdenscheid resident killed in World War I. I asked the mayor where it was. The mayor told me that the statue apparently had been torn down while Hitler was in power because it was dedicated to a Jew. However, a new monument to all of Lüdenscheid's dead from World War I did stand in its place, with Robert Stern's name listed among them.

I experienced more feelings than I can explain as I sat at receptions and concerts held in our honor in Lüdenscheid as well as Bückeburg. I had a feeling many times that people put on a smiling face at these events, but what they actually felt beneath, I could only wonder. I kept those feelings to myself, though. After all, I was their invited guest.

Yet I must say that sometimes I felt genuine warmth. Wilhelm Moskob, the wealthy florist who accompanied the mayor to New York, invited Dietrich, the reporter Eddie Graefer and his wife, and us for dinner as repayment of our hospitality the year before. They offered a sumptuous meal, but only Andy really got to eat. We had been out the night before and they had gotten a glimpse of his finicky eating habits, so they prepared some boiled chicken and vegetables to cater just to him. For us, however, they prepared the local delicacy of brook trout and toast. Evelyn and I both dislike trout, and though we picked at it to be polite, our dinner mainly consisted of toast.

One thing Evelyn did enjoy was the delicious Mosel wine. They kept pouring her one glass after another. And with every glass, her German improved. With only a couple pieces of toast to absorb what must have been an entire bottle of wine, she was stewed to the gills . . . and her German graduated from passable to fluent. At one point, Mrs. Moskob, who had taken a real shine to Andy, wanted to show him her house. Unfortunately, because Andy could not understand a word the poor woman said, the tour was going to be a bit difficult. So Evelyn agreed to accompany him, feeling quite confident in her newfound abilities to act as translator but with misplaced confidence in her ability to walk. As the tour involved going up a circular staircase to see the upstairs, it was quite a sight. Andy had to push her by the tush to get her staggering body upstairs, and then had to stand in front of her on the way down to keep her from falling on her face. Not surprisingly, Evelyn did not remember the tour in the morning.

Some of the people we bumped into on the street knew my parents and spoke highly of them. I wondered how they had spoken of my parents when the Nazis were enacting their discriminatory laws against Jews, forcing them out of the country and, later, to concentration camps. But I knew some of the expressions of happiness were genuine. At one point, Mayor Dietrich said to me there was an elderly woman who insisted on speaking to me. She must have been in her 80s at least. When I saw her, she broke down in tears. Apparently, she was one of the maids in my parents' house when I was very small. She remembered me, calling me her little Fritzen. She said she had to see me because she was so happy to finally find out that my parents and I were not killed in the concentration camps.

Not all Germans during the 1930s and 1940s were bad. The average German was a very helpless individual who, if he or she wanted to earn a living, had to be Hitler's tool. Let's face it. If you want a political job in the United States, you have to have connections. Germany back then was an extreme example. Doing the Nazis' bidding was often the difference between being employed and your family going hungry.

A week before presenting the megillah for Lüdenscheid's museum, we visited Bückeburg for its own ceremony to honor its prewar Jewish population. The idea for the ceremony had developed when Mayor Pruel met me in 1990 and learned of the ceremony at the former Lüdenscheid Jewish temple. The city council wound up inviting eight former Jewish citizens.

We nearly missed the trip for the 1991 ceremonies in Bückeburg (or Lüdenscheid). Lisa had fallen ill immediately after our 1990 visit to Germany and was soon in a wheelchair. When the invitation came in April 1991, she was hospitalized and deteriorating, and I didn't have the energy or inclination to respond. She died on July 3, and while we were sitting shiva, I remembered that the unanswered invitation was sitting on her desk. At that point, Evelyn suggested we should attend and do it as a family. With the help of Ruth Westheimer, Evelyn responded to the invitation, telling Bückeburg Stadtdirektor (City Director)

Ernst Möller what had happened to her mother and wondering whether she and Andy also could come. Evelyn then arranged the Lüdenscheid visit as well.

As much as I enjoyed showing Lüdenscheid to Evelyn and Andy, the visit to Bückeburg had much to offer, too. It was such a joy to show Evelyn and Andy where I had spent so much time as a child. I even decided to take them to the twelfth-century stone castle that was home to the kings and princes of the state of Schaumburg-Lippe. The royalty still lives there today. I took them on one of the castle tours and showed them the interior as well as the grounds. It was as beautiful as I remembered. The arched entrance of light brown stone still welcomed you to the grounds, where you could see the castle with its three tall spires and statue in front. I showed them the lake where I used to stand on a wrought iron bridge and dip my fishing pole in the water. The perfectly manicured hedges and lush green lawns were the same as when I had played there as a child. I had the run of the place back then because my grandfather and father were so active in Bückeburg.

I had hoped to meet the prince, Philipp-Ernst, at some point, as in a sense I felt personally connected to him. His uncle, Prince Adolf II, had awarded Schaumburg-Lippe's main military honor, the Cross for Loyal Service, to my father in 1916 for his service during World War I. In fact, I own a historically important family heirloom signed by Philipp-Ernst's great-grandfather, Prince Adolf Georg—an 1871 proclamation granting Jews the right to bear arms during the Franco-Prussian War. I brought the proclamation with me, asking that it be shown to the prince to help my chances of meeting him. Although he did not recognize the name Behrend, he was so ecstatic about the proclamation that he insisted on personally showing us the castle. He greeted us in the official reception room, which was dazzling with its red painted walls, gold trim, and a golden fireplace. Wearing a black suit and brown and yellow tie, he posed for pictures with Evelyn and Andy. He then took us from room to room.

Oftentimes when I visited Germany, I asked to speak to groups of young people. I felt it was important to share my story and educate them about the Jews and the Holocaust and try to address any misconceptions. I wanted to do so while I was in Bückeburg and had asked the city official Möller before we departed for Germany whether this would be possible. Shortly before we were scheduled to fly home, I received that chance as one of some invited guests who spoke to a group of 30 students at a *gymnasium,* which is the German equivalent of high school. Again, there would be headlines.

I had expected that the school would simply select one of its classes for me to meet. As it turned out, the school had handpicked a group of students who were about 16 years old to try to showcase its finest. I could tell that they had been told ahead of time to prepare some questions because their initial ones were very unnatural and abstract. But I had my own set of questions that I like to ask to try to generate a more meaningful discourse. I asked how old their fathers and grandfathers were. I also asked if any of their family members had been in Russia or France during the war. I give the students credit. They were forthcoming and told us the things their parents and grandparents had either done or allowed to happen that embarrassed them.

But we had come at an opportune time, as skinheads and neo-Nazis were causing upheaval in Germany. The Berlin Wall had just come down two years earlier, meaning not only those from the former East Germany were flooding across, but also other Eastern Europeans from the communist bloc. Physical attacks on foreigners were in the news, stirring up the world's concerns about the nation as a whole as these newcomers took jobs and caused a drain on German resources. Rather than depending solely on my recollection, in this instance, I will point you to the reporting of the local newspapers.

The *Schaumburger Land* described how one student asked the Jewish visitors to the school their thoughts about what was going on in Germany at the time. A 68-year-old woman named Herta Ermann explained how the current xenophobia compared to what Jews experienced during Hitler's reign. She said it felt like 1933 all over again and it brought back visions of storm troopers on the rampage. But sure enough, one student questioned whether the foreigners were the reason for current economic and other problems for Germans, although he was quickly reprimanded by a classmate.

While its main story covering my visit indicated things had proceeded well, Bückeburg's *General-Anzeiger* wrote a separate five-paragraph commentary that described a more heated part of the conversation. It focused on Andy posing a question to the students about what they thought about skinheads and neo-Nazis in Germany, considering that America was dealing with such individuals, too. The discussion grew sharper when one of the students said skinheads were not an issue in Germany but explained, in a nonsensical comment, that it would remain a problem in America "as long as the intelligent people [who apparently were pro-skinhead in his mind] over there weren't pushed to even more extreme behavior. Because the mass of the population, after all, is just stupid." The newspaper criticized the student, using a cliché that is popular in both English and German: "Those in glass houses shouldn't throw stones."

School officials were appalled at the student, as were the fellow students who berated him for his attitude. The student subsequently was removed from the room. But I feel the conversation with what had turned out to be skinheads was the most revealing of the trip, because it confirmed for me what I suspected all along—Nazi sympathy was still a strong undercurrent in Germany even as the broad population desired reconciliation.

Although this discussion was an extreme response, I never shied over the years from asking students about what their parents (and later, grandparents) did during the Second World War and whether they heard any stories about Hitler growing up. Especially early on, the principals of these schools sometimes would take me aside and tell me I was out of line in asking such questions of students. But I felt the questions were entirely proper. It is one thing for Germans to seek to atone for the past; it is another for them to try to remove it from their children's consciousness. Most of the early postwar textbooks seemed to have skipped right over the years 1939 to 1945. The bottom line during my visits back then was that the principals were ashamed. In contrast, I was very grateful to the good Lord that I was able to survive these horrible times so I could teach future generations and try to keep it from happening again.

In my later visits, I felt the principals were growing more open-minded. They had invited Holocaust survivors specifically to bring the conversation back to light. So there was some progress. As the years went on, and the questions became about grandparents instead of parents, however, the students tended to know less and less about their families' connections to their Nazi past. The answer was always the same when I asked what their family members did during the war. They knew very little about it. Nobody ever told them, they said.

In fact, you can hear that sentiment virtually anywhere you go in Germany. I even heard it at the Eagle's Nest, one of Hitler's former residences.

◌℞

Before I go further, let me tell you more about the Eagle's Nest, which I have visited several times. As I said before, I am quite the tourist. I do not deal in the irony of a Jew standing inside Hitler's innermost sanctum or anything like that. All I can tell you is that I wanted to show my lady friend of ten years, Theda "Teddy" Parness, some of the most impressive scenery along the German-Austrian border, and around the year 2000, I delivered.

Though actually completed the previous summer, the Eagle's Nest was commissioned by Martin Bormann, the number 2 man in the Nazi Party, for presentation to Nazi number 1 for his 50th birthday on April 20, 1939—two months after my family's escape. Bormann designed it as a retreat for Hitler and a place that would impress visiting dignitaries, serving as an extension of the Obersalzberg complex at the base of the mountain where Hitler's Berghof residence and an extensive underground bunker system were located.

Well, "impress" is not a strong enough word to describe the *Kehlsteinhaus*, as it is called in German, and the scenery of which it is part. Without seeing it, you cannot imagine the height of the building, perched atop a ridge in the Bavarian Alps at an elevation of 6,000 feet. As you ascend to the Eagle's Nest, you gain an appreciation of the engineering challenge it represented—it seems like it should have been impossible. You ride a bus along a winding road that the Germans cut through the sheer rocky slope and that includes five tunnels. Then you walk through another tunnel to a large brass elevator, the shaft of which was blasted through the heart of the mountain peak. You board the elevator and when you emerge, you are inside the chalet-like structure at the top.

A fireplace with red Italian marble, a gift from Italian dictator Benito Mussolini, catches your eye as you enter the main room. The building is a converted restaurant, and you can lose yourself in the vista by looking out the windows that surround you, or you can sit outside on the terrace, where additional tables are set up. If you are as fortunate as I was, you have the opportunity to see hang gliding enthusiasts float effortlessly through the mountain range, riding the air currents up and down for as much an hour through the high altitudes before touching down.

This visit to the Eagle's Nest was unplanned. I had taken my friend all over the world on trips, including several to Germany. On this vacation, we were planning only to tour Austria, including the town of Salzburg, which is just across the German border. Suddenly, the idea struck me. "I know you've heard so much about the Eagle's Nest," I told her. "Let me take you there."

We drove across the border to Berchtesgaden, the town at the foot of the mountains, and then ascended by car to the Obersalzberg. Finally, we took the bus for the climb to the Eagle's Nest. It was lunchtime, so I suggested we have a bite to eat.

We sat at one of the restaurant's several elongated wooden tables, perhaps 12 to 15 feet long. About 16 individuals sat around one of those tables. They ranged in age from about 30 to 50, meaning they had learned about the war years from their parents' generation. My friend and I were chatting in English, but, of course, I could understand our neighbors' conversation. Soon, my attention was aroused as I realized they were talking about Hitler and the Holocaust and, apparently, feeling they could speak unguardedly in the presence of a couple foreign tourists. It was like one of my classroom discussions, but this time without anyone holding back on how they truly felt.

"Do you really believe what has been written about Hitler's time and the concentration camps actually happened?"

Their opinions varied. Some stated emphatically that yes, these things did happen, but others expressed doubt. One even argued that Goebbels, Hitler's propaganda minister, had counterparts when it came to spinning lies about the Jews. "Germans knew that Goebbels's propaganda was exactly what it was—you couldn't believe it," he said. "Who's to say that other countries and other people cannot use propaganda in the other direction and say the opposite?"

"These things are not as bad as we've been made to believe," another added. "I cannot believe an educated and civilized people like the Germans would stoop this low, or that we would allow something like this to happen."

It was hard for me to believe the opinions of grown adults so many years after these events.

I tried to continue eating my meal, but after a while, it was difficult to digest because of what I was hearing. I began glancing their way, and from time to time, I would shake my head in disbelief. After a while, they noticed me watching them. Not only that, but they could see in my expression that I understood every word they were saying.

They began to murmur among themselves. Then, in English, a few of the men and women sitting closest started speaking to me. "We know you are speaking English," he said. "Where do you come from?"

"I come from America," I responded.

"Oh, where from in America?"

"New York," I replied.

"Oh, really, New York," the man said. "Well, I've been in New York. What a beautiful city."

Soon, the conversation shifted, as another person asked what I was doing in Germany.

"I'm a visitor," I answered. "Actually, I'm not visiting Germany. I went to Austria, but I came here because I heard so much about the Eagle's Nest."

I knew the small talk wouldn't last long. Eventually, they were going to try to get a sense of exactly how much of their conversation I had understood. I didn't want to get too deeply into it, but they persisted.

"We have the feeling that you do understand a little bit of German," someone said.

"Yes, I do," I replied. Actually, I was struggling a bit to understand their English. So at that point, I told them it would be fine to switch the conversation to German and make things easier for them.

"Where did you learn your German?" one of them asked after expressing his appreciation. "You speak a very good German."

This was uncomfortable enough already. So I spoke evasively, trying to avoid confrontation and talking about my true heritage. "Well, you know they teach German in the schools at home," I said.

They all looked at me quizzically. They were not stupid. They knew that no American-raised individual could speak German the way I do.

"Ja," the questioner responded, "but your German is not a school German. It is a different German. How do you come to your German?"

I hesitated. One last time, I tried to deflect the line of questioning. "My parents are German," I responded. "And they spoke to me in German at home."

"Well, that sounds all nice and well," he said. "However, you cannot pick up that kind of German just by speaking to your parents. Your vocabulary—it had to be schooled somewhere outside of America."

At that point, I conceded that there was, after all, a reason that my German was so true to proper form. "Well, I was very young when I left Germany," I told them, "and I did have a little bit of German schooling." The admission that I was originally German clearly startled them. Then another person asked how long I had been in America.

"I came to America when I was 13," I said.

At this point, however, I will let you in on a secret. I can take a dispassionate view about Germany most of the time, but this German tendency to deny, deny, deny what happened to the Jews is the trigger that could always set off my temper. So even though I couldn't blame them for their curiosity, my patience evaporated. My simple tourist lunch was no more. At this point, I wanted them to know the whole story, so I injected a fact that I figured would open the door for me to tell them. "I lived in Cuba for more than a year," I added.

My questioner walked through the door. "How come you went to Cuba?" he asked.

Now, I must admit that I am a loud person by nature, so loud, in fact, that my kids and my friends are always nudging me to keep my voice down. Well, no one was elbowing me right now to keep my voice down. So I was at high volume when I responded, leaving no doubt that everyone seated at the table could hear me.

"Well," I said, "it was the only country in the world that we could get to within a very short period of time for my father to be released from the concentration camp."

Then the quiet returned, turning to deathly silence. More than a half century after the Holocaust, guilt still hung thick in the former Third Reich. Now it was their turn to be at a loss for words. After an awkward pause, the silence broke.

"Well, no one realized what was happening," one of the older individuals said softly.

"Well, there were enough people who did know," I snapped.

In all my visits to my former homeland, the reaction had always been the same. "We didn't know." Now here it was again. By this point, my retort to that statement was well rehearsed. I asked them where they came from. Some said they were from Cologne, others from Stuttgart, or Düsseldorf, or Mainz.

Tempering my words with the understanding that it was their parents, not they, who were old enough to remember, I said, "I understand that you don't know firsthand. But there are many cities so close and around the various concentration camps. And you can't tell me that the odor of the gas ovens burning flesh couldn't reach anyone living in those cities."

Finally, one of them again gave the reply I had heard many times before.

"What could they have done?" someone asked.

I hate to say it, but I agree with it. After all, I may have been sheltered, but I was not completely blind to what was happening in the 1930s. For any German with the courage to question what the Nazis were doing to the Jews, the price was nearly automatic: imprisonment in the camps, perhaps death. There was not much anyone could have done by the time my family fled prior to World War II. In fact, you have to wonder what Germans with responsibility for the killings were thinking at the time. Upon entering the concentration camps, prisoners received numbers tattooed on their arms as a means to identify them. But perhaps it had another effect—easing the consciences of the murderers by letting them think in terms of eliminating numbers rather than killing people with names.

So you see, I can never harbor a grudge against the German people all these years later. Would I have visited so many times if I truly felt they were all guilty, and that their country had not made an effort to make amends?

CR

It is natural to wonder whether Germany could ever return to the 1930s. I don't think it could happen. Then again, although you have isolated, enlightened individuals who want people like me to shed light on the Holocaust, most Germans want to forget.

What was it that made the German people liable to a takeover by perhaps the most corrupt, psychotic group of individuals in the history of the world? The German people as a whole could not have been evil. Their acquiescence to the rantings of Hitler, Göring, and Goebbels had to come from somewhere.

Partly, I can tell you from firsthand memories that there was deep resentment with how Germany was treated by the Allies after losing the First World War. The German economy was laid bare by the reparations owed to the victors laid out in the Treaty of Versailles. Industries could not be rebuilt because the Allies took away German factories' machinery as loot. Hitler came to power with a focus on rebuilding industry and creating employment for the German people.

The difficult part to understand, however, is why Germans went along with the Nazis' thuggery and discriminatory tactics. To me, the answer comes from a common German trait. They were followers. They were always followers. They followed the flag, they followed their Kaiser, and then they followed Hitler.

When somebody told them what to do in a loud enough voice, they would click their heels, stand at attention, and do what they were told. They were very much influenced by authority. They would never think of even questioning why they should do something. It is not how they were constituted. I think that trait still remains.

I can remember a trip with Lisa to Europe when we took a train from Zurich to Vienna. We had first-class tickets and expected special treatment. Yet at the German border, the very first time one of the customs agents opened the door to our compartment, he didn't ask for passports. He demanded them, yelling, "Passports!" It was the same as I remembered in February 1939, when we were finally allowed to board our ship, after Germany officials had shouted at us and berated us. They were just doing their job. But the way it came out of their mouths made you shudder.

Germans were also patriots of the highest order. They would gladly give their life for the fatherland. The Jews were no different at the time. They were the first ones to go to war in defense of the fatherland, as shown by my mother's first husband and my father. My father and plenty of other German Jews in New York had it ingrained in them to take pride in how the Wehrmacht fought as they conquered western Europe and advanced into Russia in the east.

The lies in the Nazis' propaganda newspaper, Der Stürmer, which displayed horrible caricatures of Jews with hooked noses and more, were outrageous, saying how the Jews were taking advantage of the Aryans, getting the best jobs, owning the biggest stores, and amassing the most money. I would argue that the vast majority of the population knew it was outrageous. They didn't go along with the Nazis on the Jewish question out of any innate belief. They went along out of fear. My parents' business in Lüdenscheid never suffered from the propaganda. Germans still came in and bought their silk and bedding as if nothing happened until the Nazis eventually left my parents no choice but to close. In fact, business tended to pick up at night, as people were scared of the Nazis, but not too scared to sneak in to make their purchases when it was dark.

Not only that, but my father had more non-Jewish friends than Jewish ones. He played Skat regularly on Saturday nights. They would drink to all hours at the local tavern. The head of the police department and the priest from the local church were part of the group. So I can't see the propaganda having had any real effect on them.

CB

The astounding thing that happened after the war is that some German Jews actually did go back to Germany to live after all the horrors of World War II. I suppose my best explanation is that they felt more at home there than they did in the United States. Now for an American, that is very difficult to understand. But if a fellow was brought up in the Deep South in Mississippi or Alabama and his boss transferred him to New York City, he would be very unhappy there and want to go back. This was no different.

Although some Jews returned, Judaism as a whole was stagnant in Germany for many years. But it is coming back. According to the Virtual Jewish Library, about 119,000 Jews live in Germany, representing the eighth-largest population in the world, although a far cry from the 550,000 who lived there in 1933. The Jewish communities have rebuilt beautiful temples in Munich and Berlin. I am not so sure I would consider it a sign of reconciliation. In fact, large numbers of Jews in Germany now are refugees who fled the former Soviet Union, meaning their motivations were much different for living there. But I suppose it is one small step along the path, although antisemitic attacks in France and elsewhere frighteningly have been on the rise of late.

CHAPTER 10

Looking Back

The first service call was as ordinary as could be. The second—thanks to my accent and the fragrant Cuban cigar belonging to what turned out to be one of the most distinguished gentlemen I ever met—would change my life and prove one of the key reasons I decided to write this book.

It began one day in the late 1970s with a phone call from a Mrs. Moyers. She said I came highly recommended and wanted me to give a price on installing air conditioning in her new apartment on Central Park West. So I came over and took a look at the apartment, which had no furniture and bare walls, and told her I would get back to her. But she wanted a favor. While she was not worried about getting a fair price, she said she would appreciate it if I would look at the apartment again when her husband returned from an overseas business trip so he would be part of the decision. I said that wasn't a problem and ended up coming back a couple weeks later.

When I returned, I was transfixed. There was beautiful furniture throughout the apartment. More impressively, pictures of kings and queens, as well as presidents and prime ministers, hung everywhere on the walls. Winston Churchill, John F. Kennedy, and Lyndon Johnson were just some of the world leaders gazing down at this wide-eyed air conditioning man. And her husband was standing alongside them in the pictures.

"Where did you meet all these people?" I asked her husband in wonderment.

"I met them when I worked in the Kennedy administration and when I was press secretary for Johnson," Bill Moyers replied.

Then I asked him where he had been on his business trip. He told me he had been in Cuba for his job as a journalist. Considering I had never heard of him, I didn't realize he was well known and had a show on PBS called *Bill Moyers Journal*.

"Oh, now I know where you got your Cuban cigar," I said.

"How you do know it's a Cuban cigar?" he asked.

"Well, before I came to the United States, I lived for over a year in Cuba, and I know what a Cuban cigar looks like and what it smells like. Aside from the fact that I smoke myself."

Well, that statement caught his attention. Now he asked for the whole story of where I came from and how I got to the United States, because he knew for sure my accent was not Cuban.

"That's a *long* story!" I told Moyers. "And I have other customers."

"That's OK, just tell me the short version," he said.

I kept protesting, but he refused to take no for an answer. So I told him about being born in Germany. I told him about Kristallnacht, of my father's detention in Sachsenhausen, and how my mother secured his release by proving we would leave Germany as soon as possible. When that wasn't enough to satisfy him, I told him how we escaped to Cuba with my Uncle Otto's help, how I had my bar mitzvah there, and how we came to the United States after nearly a year and a half of waiting for our quota number to be called. The conversation must have lasted at least 15 to 20 minutes.

When I finished, he said, "You must be very grateful to this country for allowing you entry."

That statement took me by surprise. I suppose it is a reasonable assumption that many people would make, but that is never the view I took.

"Mr. Moyers, the United States should be the one that's grateful," I said. "*It* should be grateful that it was the choice of the cream of European intelligentsia. The doctors, scientists, writers, and artists who adopted this country made it what it is today. Our achievements in the fields of health, space, and literature would not have been possible were it not for those that made this country their home."

This time, Moyers was the one caught off guard. But after a moment to absorb what I had just said, I could see from his face that he was formulating an idea in his mind. When he told me what it was, I was floored.

"Let me ask you something," he said. "Would you allow me to interview you on a program I have on television?"

I was flattered, but it didn't take long for me to say no. "My opinions may not be the same that my customers would like to hear," I said. "If when I retire you're still interested, I'd be more than happy to."

He reluctantly accepted my answer and, no, he never kept track to see when I retired. I won't hold it against him, though. I think he's been busy.

I filed that conversation away for perhaps 25 years. But you never know what happens once a seed is planted. In 2003, I started speaking at my synagogue in Scarsdale, New York. Considering you've read this far, you've probably already figured out what happened next. Once I started talking, I couldn't shut up. I haven't since. I enjoy speaking to both young people and adults, and I enjoy the conversations that result. I've spoken in front of public schools, Jewish groups, and practically anyone else who wants to hear my tale, including the governor of New Jersey. I feel compelled to ensure the world never forgets about the Holocaust, and I feel it is important to share my perspective because, as Moyers discovered, it varies so much from other people of my generation. Ultimately, that desire contributed to me writing this book.

Before I go further, however, I need to take a moment to give Mr. Moyers his due. As we wrapped up our conversation, he asked what my favorite cigar brand was. I told him I didn't prefer the Cuban brands because they're too heavy. I preferred a Belgian cigar called H. Upmann. He informed me that was one of his favorites, too. He said he was leaving for Belgium in a few weeks and would bring a box back for me. I thanked him, certain that the promise would be forgotten the second that the door closed behind him.

A few weeks later, a gentleman entered my store holding a box. Now I must admit that my memory for faces and names is terrible, to the point of being embarrassing at times. This turned out to be one of those times.

"Hi, Fred, how are you?" the man asked. "Remember I promised you something?"

"You did?" I responded with a puzzled expression.

Then he lightly tossed the package down on a chair with a grin. The label on the box said "H. Upmann."

"Oh my God, Mr. Moyers?" I said, my face turning a deep shade of red.

"Bet you thought I had forgotten about it!" he exclaimed with a hearty laugh.

"Now I remember! In my wildest dream, I never thought you'd remember to bring me a box of cigars—not only that, but the kind I asked for," I said.

That, to me, is a great man—someone with fame and power who does not act as if he is better than everyone else.

"Well, anybody that brings me cigars, I will never forget the name," I added.

ରେ

I can tell you quite a bit about how the experiences of prewar Germany and the Holocaust changed me. But sometimes, I think what matters most are the things that never change, the ones that keep you centered even when a world full of chaos surrounds you. Being Jewish means belonging to a heritage. In my case, my heritage and family are inextricably bound together through the centuries. No matter what the Nazis took from us before we boarded the *Iberia*, they couldn't touch that.

Many third- and fourth-generation Americans are fortunate if they know the name of even one ancestor who lived in the old country. I cannot imagine my grandchildren and their grandchildren having such a problem. That's because we have *Unsere Familien-Chronik*—our family chronicle. I shudder as I think how one man, Adolf Hitler, nearly succeeded in ending this proud Behrend family heritage. But he did not. The chronicle goes on. The announcement published in the *Aufbau* upon my father's death in 1958 at age 75 explains to perfection my family's dedication to its heritage: "He was a worthy descendant of a family that for more than ten generations was typical of the patriarchal beauty and purity of family life, the profound Jewishness and the impeccable moral conduct of German Jews. He was sure that his son will continue to write and to live *Unsere Familien-Chronik.*"

That might sound like a lot of weight to put on a young guy's shoulders, but I didn't mind. In my later years, in fact, the chronicle has become an obsession. I stay up late at night, far later than any right-minded man of my age ought to, translating the time-worn, handwritten pages. You should see me dash up the stairs when I get the urge to start working, zooming right past the chairlift installed in my New Jersey townhouse.

The fascination stems largely from the fact that the handwritten document dates back to 1490, two years before Columbus sailed for America. Let me put it to you this way. If you have ever tried to read the Declaration of Independence in the original script, with the letter S looking like an F and so many words being spelled differently than they are today, you get an idea of how difficult it is to read the chronicle in its old German. (It could have been worse. The original script consisted of German written in Hebrew characters. In 1893, the family hired someone to translate it into German characters.)

The chronicle goes back through the centuries to the very beginning for the Behrends. The first substantive entries state that between 1540 and 1560, the family bought a house in the village of Rodenberg, which is about 20 miles east of where my grandparents lived in Bückeburg. Additions were made over the centuries, including stables, a smokehouse, and a carriage house. I don't know what eventually became of the house, but it still stood into the early 1900s.

The document describes how members of my family served a central religious role in the village. They often led services, singing melodies handed down through the generations. An ancestor named Jacob paid to have 30 calf hides turned into parchment, and then hired a rabbi in a nearby village to scribe one Sefer Torah (Torah scroll) and one megillah. In 1804, his son Ahron sold another 30 hides for the same purpose. These were placed to use in the local synagogue. "For a synagogue to have its own Sefer Torah was a great mitzvah," the chronicle says. "A period of three days feasting was solemnly begun. The last day, a great meal was served. It is called the Sefer Torah meal."

Another lesson from the chronicle is the changing view of Germany's Jews toward their rulers over time. While my father felt he was German first, this attitude among the Jews of the various German provinces and duchies was a phenomenon that was only 125 years old when Hitler came to power. On May 13, 1800, the feelings of Jews toward the fatherland differed greatly. On that date, the chronicle states, all Jewish males between 15 and 40 were ordered to report to the landgrave (a position of German nobility) for induction into the army. Knowing the landgrave would be away for a few days, congregation leaders accompanied these men and bribed a lower official to gain their freedom, receiving special dispensation from the local rabbi to travel on the holiday of Shavuot when Jewish law would normally forbid it.

"Nothing was impossible for us Jews in these days as long as the payoff was placed in the proper hands," the chronicle states. "These bribes of the counts, barons, and landgraves to keep us from serving in the military should in no way be construed as cowardice. The result of hundreds of years of abuse, intolerance, pressure, and hate that we suffered by the hands of our sovereigns did not warrant our loyalty, love for fatherland, or patriotism. We were never citizens but rather always put below the common farm animals."

But change was coming for German Jews, through a man widely viewed in history as a tyrant. In January 1808, Napoleon Bonaparte's armies marched through the region. Jews there would come to consider him a liberator as he spread the ideals of the French Revolution. Napoleon installed his youngest brother Jérôme as king of Westphalia, which was created from several states and principalities in northwestern Germany. He instructed his brother to free the Jews from the onerous taxes once paid to the reigning monarch for the right to live in the local fiefdom. Napoleon also gave Jews the right to take up any trade they wished and live anywhere they chose.

"Is it small wonder therefore that we look upon Napoleon as our Messiah?" the chronicle reads. "Though his thirst for conquest was insatiable, to us he was a great man who cleaned the morass of centuries of unjust taxes, laws, and persecution."

In fact, our family has always sung one particular Hebrew psalm on the Sabbath to the melody of "La Marseillaise," the French national anthem. My father didn't know for sure the origins of the melody but assumed it dated back to the time of Napoleon's conquest of Germany.

Napoleon also gave Jews the right to bear surnames for the first time. A story handed down through the generations is that when the time came for my ancestors to pick a family name, their choice was made easy by a wrought iron sign hanging over the front door in Rodenberg in the shape of a bear (baer in German). From baer, the name Behrend evolved.

One other point that the chronicle tells us about regards the religious artifacts still in my family's possession today, including our centuries-old Seder plate. I also have instruments used for many decades in the Jewish circumcision (bris) ritual. In the 1800s, family members began to serve as mohels to oversee the passing along of God's covenant as mandated in the Torah, with a book recording each bris performed.

∞

Although the chronicle shows the importance of family heritage in Jewish life, it is not all just history. The stories told in this book and others are part of that chronicle too, as will be future ones of my children and grandchildren. My story is not just one of escaping Germany, but of the years that followed, full of family and friends, enjoyed in a life lived with Jewish values. Over the years, the Boots and Poles gang got together so often, at Lake Oscawana and otherwise, that the bonds grew of friendship grew as close as family and sometimes deeper. When a friend's parent died, it got to the point that they usually didn't want a rabbi to preside over the funeral service. They would almost always tell the funeral director that they wanted a graveside service and that I would conduct it. Many of these old friends such as Freddy Westheimer are gone now. I spoke at their services as well.

These lifelong bonds reward you in unexpected ways. One of the most touching moments in my life came in 1991. Everyone had headed for their houses along Lake Oscawana for the annual Fourth of July get-together of the Boots and Poles gang. That year, on July 3, my wife died after her long illness. Somebody called one of our friends, who immediately called all the others. And they all turned back. My house in Yonkers was absolutely filled with people. My children and I didn't have to cook for a week. They took care of our every need.

As Lisa's health deteriorated, I lost interest in owning a business anymore. I decided to sell to whoever made anything resembling a decent offer. So I did, although it turned out to be something of a mistake, as it took six years of litigation just to collect a fraction of the sale price. But with the business gone, I decided it was to time to spend my winters in the Florida apartment that Lisa and I had bought ten years earlier to use for vacations with the kids. Speaking to children and adults about the Holocaust or my immigrant life was something that never crossed my mind. I eyed retirement, relaxation, palm trees, and as little cold weather as possible.

CR

But perhaps I should have known all along that I wouldn't be able to keep my thoughts to myself for long. I hadn't realized it at the time, but a preview of my second "career" had come at Genesis Agudas Achim, the synagogue near my home in Yonkers, before I sold the business. When the rabbis were away, I used to give the *D'var Torah* to comment on the day's Torah portion. This time, I added my own twist. One day, the rabbi left the dais and said, "Today we're not going to give a sermon. Today I'm going to ask a question. What made you come to shul today?"

People gave all kinds of corny or sentimental reasons. Finally, he asked me.

"Rabbi, you don't want to know," I said.

"Yes, I do want to know," he replied.

"Rabbi, you're going to be sorry if you ask me," I insisted.

But he insisted. So I told him.

"I had a lousy week in business," I said. "The people that came into my store, they were the biggest pains in the ass you ever did see. I would love to choke them or kick them out of the store, but you know you can't do that. So now I had a big choice. One of my customers is a psychiatrist and he always told me that if I ever needed him, he wouldn't charge me much. I could've gone to the psychiatrist, paid him $100, or I could come to shul over here and sit and relax a bit and forget the past week. So I figured I'll take the $100 from one pocket, put it in the other pocket, and get the same service."

The rabbi said, "That's the first true answer I heard today."

Then, he added, "But you could have contributed the $100 from the other pocket."

My retirement continued with a spiel here and there to the congregation during the warmer weather, and relaxing in the Florida warmth during winter. But as years passed, informal talks there and later at Shaarei Tikvah in Scarsdale became more of a regular thing instead of the occasional Sabbath speech. Then one day, the rabbi was going to Germany on sabbatical to study to write a thesis. It would mark a turning point as, to help him with thesis, I provided him my father's diary (written as part of the family chronicle). Word about the thesis and the diary got around. On one Shabbat morning after services, we were having a study session. Someone mentioned the thesis. People wanted to know two things: how I got my name and details about how Jews lived in the olden days of Germany. So I started talking about the history of some of my relatives, why the German Jews were so grateful to Napoleon, and that we sing a psalm to the melody of "La Marseillaise." Soon I was holding lectures on one topic after another. I haven't stopped since.

It still amazes me how I can have trouble remembering something that happened last week, yet experiences from my childhood can still come back to me as vividly as if they happened yesterday. I can still see those Cologne synagogues on fire and the prayer books and tallitot thrown on the street. And I understand now how sheltered I was. Any other child would have been far more frightened than I was that day. I just did not know enough about what was going on to understand. Although my parents hid so much from me about the Nazis until we left Germany, I don't resent it. I would do the same thing under those circumstances with my child. You want to shield your children as long as you can.

Even now, though, I still have pangs of a lost childhood. In Lüdenscheid, my mother took me to public school and back, leaving me no interaction with the other children as the antisemitic edicts came more frequently and with greater severity. In Cologne, I had the company of Cantor Baum's two children, but before I had much chance to enjoy that friendship, Kristallnacht took it away and forced me to grow up.

These memories are all things that I can share. I tell it to children in one way, to adults in another. But everyone can learn the lessons of Kristallnacht. There are lessons to be learned from my family's chronicle and Judaica, too, in particular how Judaism can create unbreakable bonds from grandparent to parent to child.

CR

If I was busy in retirement in Yonkers, I was busier upon moving to be near my children in Voorhees, New Jersey. My activity accelerated in 2008 while spending a few free moments at what is now called the Esther Raab Holocaust Museum and Goodwin Education Center, located inside the Jewish Community Center (JCC) in neighboring Cherry Hill. A female JCC staff member was talking to a group of children about the museum's various artifacts, including the yellow star that Jews were forced to wear on their clothes. She sensed I had more than a passing interest and said, "I think there's somebody here who might have a better explanation of this." Once I explained my history to her, she sent me to the office of the person who oversees educational programs for the museum. Soon enough, I had agreed to speak about the Holocaust to schools throughout South Jersey.

That fall, the head of the Jewish Federation of South Jersey asked if I would like to go to the statehouse in Trenton to speak at a statewide event hosted by then-governor Jon Corzine, commemorating the seventieth anniversary of Kristallnacht. I gave them my firsthand account of the burning synagogues in Cologne and told them of my father's arrest in Lüdenscheid and detention in Sachsenhausen. More than 200 individuals, including Holocaust survivors, attended that event. "Hatred is a learned behavior," I told the gathering. "Don't be a follower of bigotry. Be a leader against it. Until hatred and bigotry no longer exist in this world, the meaning of the words 'never again' can never be realized."

We live in a chaotic world. Even the worst crime in the history of humanity, the Holocaust, has not cured the world of its ills. Genocides still occur. They have happened in the Sudan. They have happened in Rwanda. Anyone could wonder what kind of God would let this happen, and I don't have an answer. What I do know is everybody has to believe in something. I don't care if you believe in Allah. I don't care if you believe in Jesus Christ. I don't care if you believe in Buddha. You have to believe in something. Having something to pass down b'chol dor vador is what sustains us. It surely sustained my family from the Final Solution to the New World.

As so much of this book has been about Passover, I feel it appropriate to tell you one last Seder remembrance. In an entry to my father's diary on my twentieth birthday in 1946, he wrote about Abraham's jewel, which in talmudic tradition was worn around the patriarch's neck to protect him upon leaving his parents' home. This passage was something that he read during a Seder:

> Before Abraham left his parental home, God hung a jewel around his neck that possessed the strange power, to greet Abraham with love, respect and friendship where ever he wandered. . . .

> It therefore must be, that the good Lord in his infinite wisdom provided you with the same precious amulet given to Abraham to work its marvels and

miracles for you. May he never remove this magical amulet from your neck, that you may look to a carefree, happy and blessed future.

I do feel that my life has been truly blessed in such a manner and that this amulet will sustain us b'chol dor vador. In fact, one type of "amulet" survived from Germany and passed from my father, to me, and then to my children and grandchildren. It is a yad, which literally means "hand" in English and is a Jewish ritual item used for pointing to the words when reading the Torah. It was during Kristallnacht, hours before my father's arrest and detainment in Sachsenhausen, while he wandered the streets of Lüdenscheid after the Nazis' night of ransacking, that he found the long, silver item lying on the ground. He picked it up and placed it in his coat pocket.

Fortunately, the gestapo did not consider the tarnished item worth confiscating. It survived and made it with our other belongings out of Europe. It was used in 1939 in Cuba at my bar mitzvah, and again when Andy and Evelyn were called to the Torah for their ceremonies. In 2014, 76 years after Kristallnacht, at our synagogue of Congregation Beth El, with tears in my eyes, I handed it to my granddaughter Marisa. The yad was in the same shape that it was when my father found it. Purposely, I have never polished it so that it looks the same as it did on that fateful day. As she read from the Holy Scriptures, I felt my father's approving presence once more.